Tintin

Tintin

Jean-Marc and Randy Lofficier

www.pocketessentials.com

This edition published in 2011 by Pocket Essentials,
a division of Oldcastle Books
P.O.Box 394, Harpenden, Herts, AL5 1XJ
www.pocketessentials.com

A CIP catalogue record for this book is available from the British Library.

ISBN
978-1-84243-608-0 (Print)
978-1-84243-609-7 (kindle)
978-1-84243-610-3 (epub)
978-1-84243-611-0 (pdf)

2 4 6 8 10 9 7 5 3 1

Typeset by Avocet Typeset, Chilton, Aylesbury, Bucks
Printed and bound by CPI Group (UK) Ltd, Croydon, CR0 4YY

With thanks to
Ivan Noerdinger, Benoît Peeters, Philippe Goddin

Contents

CONTENTS

Tintin – Reporter of the Twentieth-century

"In the end, you know, my only international rival is Tintin! We're both little guys who don't let the big guys walk all over them. You don't see it because of my height."

Charles de Gaulle (1890–1970)[1]

The silhouette of Tintin – a young man wearing golf pants running with a white fox terrier by his side – is easily one of the most recognisable visual icons of the modern world, as much as Mickey Mouse's ears or Snoopy playing World War One ace on his doghouse.

Tintin was born – or made his first public appearance – in Belgium on 10 January 1929. Some sociologists argue that the twentieth century really began only after World War One, and that would indeed make Tintin a child of the last century. His putative birth occurred mere months before the Great Depression,

---

[1] "Au fond, vous savez, mon seul rival international, c'est Tintin! Nous sommes les petits qui ne se laissent pas avoir par les grands. On ne s'en aperçoit pas, à cause de ma taille." Charles de Gaulle according to André Malraux; source: official Charles de Gaulle site: http://www.charles-de-gaulle.com.

and a decade before World War Two, two of the twentiethth century's defining events.

To put this into the context of comics' history, *Tintin* was created the same year that American cartoonist Elzie Segar created the spinach-chewing *Popeye*, and artist Dick Calkins drew the adventures of *Buck Rogers*, adapted by Phil Nowlan from his own science fiction story. The notion that *Tintin* is, in fact, nine years older than *Superman* and ten years older than *Batman* usually causes mild cultural shock on both sides of the Atlantic, even among the most educated comics fans, who somehow regard the character as timeless.

It is that very timelessness that makes *Tintin* the perfect symbol of the twentieth century, a true witness to our era, spotlighting with astonishing 20/20 clarity all the high points of our recent history: Tintin was a Western European coloniser in Africa in the 1930s; he battled bootleggers in Chicago during Prohibition and fought alongside the Chinese against the Japanese; he walked on the moon; and in the 1970s he sided with South American guerrillas. Tintin always fitted in; anywhere, anywhen. And more so, he always made us aware that there were two sides to every story and did it with a smile.

When we read *Tintin*, we simultaneously hold two images in our minds: the image we see and Hergé's amazingly symbolic vision. Apollo XII and Professor Calculus' red & white chequered rocket become inseparable from each other in our collective photo album. The story of Tintin is the story of our times.

When symbols pass away, the outpouring of grief is

out of proportion with the actual event, because people do not mourn the person who died but the part of themselves that is floating away on the river of time. On 3 May 1983, when Tintin's creator, Hergé, passed away at age 76, for many it was Tintin who died that day. It symbolised to all who had shared in the young reporter's adventures that a portion of their lives had suddenly come to an end.

The leading French and Belgian newspapers devoted their front pages to the news, illustrating it with the by-then famous panel culled from *Tintin In Tibet* showing Tintin shedding a tear over the seeming death of his friend Tchang, or the one where Snowy stands over his master's unconscious body. Tintin mourned his father; fans mourned Hergé.

Never had the passing of a cartoonist – other than perhaps that of Walt Disney – generated as much public grief and news stories, a vibrant testimony to the deep and everlasting importance of *Tintin* in French-speaking culture.

When one first looks at *Tintin*, there may be a tendency to dismiss it as being simplistic. It is, after all, supposed to be a story for children. But as one begins reading, the clarity and expressiveness of the design is revealed, almost like a blurred image slowly coming into focus. Very few artists ever had Hergé's ability to blend coherent storytelling, depth of characterisation and outstanding expression of emotion in such a fashion.

Contemporary comics scholars like to point at the progress made by comics in becoming more 'adult' (whatever that means) in the recent past by rightly singling out the works of writers such as Alan Moore, Neil Gaiman or Los Brothers Hernandez. But in fact, the *Tintin* comics were the first to have 'gone adult'. As early as 1934, encouraged by his friend, Chinese student Tchang Tchong-Jen, Hergé had plunged his hero into the midst of the Japanese invasion of China. The publication of *The Blue Lotus* in the pages of a Belgian newspaper provoked the ire of Japanese officials and several personalities protested the alleged harm done by Hergé to Nippo-Belgian relations. Conversely, the artist was invited to China by Tchang Kai-Chek's wife. No comic since then has ever provoked so much interest or controversy from the adult world, or has been treated as seriously as *The Blue Lotus* was in 1934.

And no comics writer or artist has been called before a tribunal to explain and justify his work, as Hergé was after the war, when the authorities of a newly-liberated Belgium questioned his book *The Shooting Star*. Drawn in Nazi-occupied Belgium for a Nazi-sympathetic newspaper, the book happened to give all the good roles to the pro-Axis and neutral states, while making America into a villain.

For good and bad, Hergé blazed a trail – his comics were not only 'adult', they were the product of adult choices, reflected adult concerns, were read by adults and ultimately judged by adults. Can that be said about any other comic works or creators?

Artistically, *Tintin* was the first comic ever to offer its reader a fully self-contained, totally coherent fantasy universe. Long before the intricate universes of Marvel Comics and its rivals, Hergé had built a rich and complex world centred around a simple hero, a teenage reporter – not unlike Clark Kent – flanked by his faithful pet and which included a gallery of wonderful supporting characters. The humanity of Haddock, the eccentricities of Calculus, the goofiness of the Thompsons, the mercurial nature of the Castafiore and the obnoxiousness of Jolyon Wagg become more familiar to us than the antics of our own relatives. The Tintin Family forms a Human Comedy that rivals that of Balzac.

The Tintin Universe is also comprised of a veritable atlas of imaginary countries, from Syldavia in the Balkans, to San Theodoros in South America and Khemed in the Middle East. They become shadow versions of Hitler's Germany, Nicaragua or Saudi Arabia, according to the changing needs of the times. As the twentieth century changes, so do the *Tintin* books.

As a result, both the literary reputation of *Tintin* and its popular image were not the product of a fixed or stabilised set of works, as is usually the case, but rather of a complex interplay of the same works set against a variety of different cultural and ideological backgrounds.

Tintin acquired its mythic status because it created an illusion of reality in its readers' minds, very much as JRR Tolkien's *The Lord of the Rings* or JK Rowling's Harry Potters have. Every facet of the mundane world becomes transformed by and finds its equivalent in the underlying truth of the imaginary world. However, where the other two writers succeeded because of their prose, Hergé achieved his success through the symbolic power and visual clarity of his art.

Hergé's style is concerned with finding the right line that embodies the right expression, the right movement, the right shape. It is a quest for the essential and simple truth that lies under the cumbersome trappings of the mundane, and can only be revealed through clarity and focus. His visual approach incorporates the influences of both Western Masters, such as George McManus, and traditional Chinese brush technique. Like another modern comics artist whose work also hangs in museums today, Charles Schultz, Hergé understood that less is more.

In Europe, Hergé's artistic influence cannot be underestimated. His style became a school – the so-called 'Clear Line' style, which now includes Dutch artist Joost Swarte, French artists Yves Chaland, Serge Clerc, Floc'h and Ted Benoit, and Spanish artist Daniel Torres.

There is yet one other, possibly even more important, aspect of *Tintin*'s history that makes it the most important comic series in Europe, possibly in the world – the business factor.

The concept of collecting comics and publishing them as children's books was a new one in 1930. With the publication of collected editions dubbed "albums", comics creators were guaranteed a place on the bookshelves and royalties for years to come. They were then motivated to produce their best work on a schedule that ensured quality of craftsmanship.

In America, by contrast, the syndicates which owned the comics, treated them as a disposable item, read today, gone tomorrow, a mere circulation-boosting device for throwaway newspapers, not worthy of book publication. And even if they had deemed them good material for books, the men who owned the syndicates were not book publishers and there was no synergy to be had. As a result, American creators were forced to toil deprived of artistic respectability and financial security.

The face of European comics would have been different if Hergé had relinquished his ownership of *Tintin* – as he could have. Luckily for him, the owners of *Le Vingtième Siècle*, the newspaper which first published *Tintin*, were Catholic priests who sought to evangelise, not squeeze a buck out of every venture. If not, things may have well turned out differently. But whatever the reasons, it was *Tintin*'s success in the bookstores and its creator ownership that virtually gave birth to the entire European comics publishing industry.

And ultimately, perhaps that was its most significant contribution to the History of Comics.

Hergé – I Am Tintin

'It's quite simple really, and at the same time rather complicated.'

Captain Haddock – *Land of Black Gold*.

Hergé was born Georges Rémi in Etterbeek, a suburb of Brussels, on 22 May 1907, to Alexis and Lisa Rémi. Alexis worked in the children's clothing business and his twin brother, Léon, in military uniforms. The identity of Alexis and Léon's father remained a mystery – their mother had them out of wedlock – and neither Georges, nor his younger brother, Paul, born in 1912, ever knew their paternal grandfather.

According to Hergé's later recollections, his parents used to give him a pencil and paper to keep him quiet and out of mischief, and this is how he came to discover his passion and talent for drawing. The margins of his school books became filled with art and the adventures of a small boy fighting against the German soldiers of World War One.

Young Georges spent his teenage years at the Catholic school of the Institut Saint-Boniface and received excellent grades, although paradoxically not in art classes. He joined the Catholic Scouting Federation and eventually became 'Curious Fox', the leader of the Squirrel Troop. Scout summer camp activities included group travel to Spain, Austria, Switzerland and Italy, which opened up Georges' horizons and gave him his first taste of adventure. It was also during his scout years that Georges acquired a romantic interest in the Native Americans.

The experience of being a scout became a dominant factor during Georges' crucial, formative years. When the young man's artistic skills blossomed, it was natural that his first outlet was his school's scout magazine, *Jamais Assez* (*Never Enough*), to which he began contributing illustrations, including a travelogue of a school trip to the Tyrol, in 1922.

In 1923, René Weverbergh of the Belgian national scout publication *Le Boy-Scout*, invited Georges to contribute illustrations to that magazine as well. His first professionally published illustration appeared in February 1923. He coined the pseudonym 'Hergé' – a reversal of his initials G R – almost two years later, in December 1924.

In 1925, following a recommendation by Weverbergh, the 18-year-old Georges was hired by the Catholic newspaper *Le Vingtième Siècle* (*The Twentieth Century*), which was edited by an entrepreneurial and enthusiastic priest, Abbott Norbert Wallez. Georges was hired in a minor administrative capacity and put to work in the subscription department – but that did not stop 'Curious Fox', or Hergé, as he now regularly signed his work, from continuing to contribute to *Le Boy-Scout*, by then retitled *Le Boy-Scout Belge* (*The Belgian Boy-Scout*).

In 1926, military service beckoned. Georges went in the army as an ordinary foot soldier and emerged a year later as a reserve lieutenant before returning to another kind of active duty at *Le Vingtième Siècle*. Meanwhile, in July 1926, he begun *Les Aventures de Totor, Chef de Patrouille des Hannetons* (*The Adventures of Totor, Scout Leader of the Beetle Troop*) in *Le Boy-Scout Belge*.

At the end of 1928, Wallez asked Georges Rémi to edit a weekly children's supplement, to be entitled *Le Petit Vingtième* (*The Little Twentieth Century*), fashioned after the American model. At that time, Rémi was performing various editorial tasks, contributing illustrations etc., for the magazine, while continuing to freelance for *Le Boy-Scout Belge*. He was also engaged to Germaine Kieckens, Wallez's secretary.

The first issue of *Le Petit Vingtième* came out on 1 November 1928. At first, Hergé merely illustrated *Les Aventures de Flup, Nenesse, Poussette et Cochonnet*, a strip written by another of the paper's journalists. But in issue 11, on 10 January 1929, he launched his own series, *Tintin In the Land of the Soviets*, at first a remake of *Totor* in a slightly different context – Totor was a scout, Tintin a cub reporter.

A year later, on 23 January 1930, Hergé created *Quick & Flupke*, two Brussels street urchins whose nemesis is Agent No. 15, a brave policeman who looks exactly like the Thompsons.

Hergé became aware of Tintin's growing popularity after a publicity stunt planned by the editors of *Le Vingtième Siècle*. Upon the conclusion of the first story on 8 May 1930 it was announced in the paper that he and Tintin – in reality, a child made up to look like the character – would arrive from Russia at Brussels' rail station. Hergé thought no one would show up; instead, he and his companion were greeted by nearly a thousand screaming children.

By the end of the year, *Tintin* was collected in book form, albeit only by *Le Petit Vingtième*, and was published in France in the prestigious *Coeurs Vaillants* magazine. Hergé had become a star. In 1932, he married Germaine and signed a better contract with Belgian publisher Casterman, who would ensure that his books received a greater distribution.

In 1934, Hergé had another dramatic encounter: that of Tchang Tchong-Jen, a Chinese student at the Fine Arts Academy of Brussels. Tchang not only helped him with the research necessary to make Tintin's fifth adventure *The Blue Lotus* a better book, even drawing the Chinese ideograms used in the story, but he also introduced Hergé to the techniques of inking with a brush, and the importance of injecting a sense of realism in the story to balance its fantasy.

The publication of *The Blue Lotus* also made Hergé realise how important he and Tintin had become. Because of its pro-Chinese slant, the story provoked angry reactions from Japanese officials and other personalities. *Le Vingtième Siècle*'s new editor, Schmidt, asked Hergé to change his story, but bolstered by Tchang, the artist refused to back down and fought to retain his independence; he won.

In 1934, Hergé created the 'Atelier Hergé,' a small art studio designed to handle the, by then, numerous requests to create commercial and advertising illustrations. He launched a new comics series in *Le Petit Vingtième*, a funny animal adventure entitled *Popol & Virginie Chez les Lapinos*, a parody western in which two pooh bears go to live among Indian rabbits in the Far West.

In 1936, Hergé created yet one more comics series, *Jo, Zette & Jocko*, this time at the request of Abbott Courtois, the editor of *Coeurs Vaillants*, who had expressed the desire to see a series featuring real children with a real family. Jo and Zette were the children of Engineer Legrand, and Jocko was their pet monkey. Two double-length *Jo, Zette & Jocko* sagas were published between 1936 and 1939, the first dealing with a mad scientist seeking to conquer the world from an underwater base, the second with a futuristic stratospheric plane.

During that time, *Tintin* books were produced like clockwork, one after the other. Even Germaine occasionally assisted with the inking of her husband's work. This golden age of Hergé's career came to an end in 1939.

That year, as rumours of war intensified, Hergé was mobilised and sent into the army. Nevertheless, he continued to work diligently. In early 1940 he became sick and was sent home for health reasons. In May, the Germans invaded Belgium. On 9 May 1940, *Le Vingtième Siècle* and its weekly children's supplement were discontinued. As a direct consequence, Tintin's ninth adventure *Land of Black Gold* was left uncompleted. The darkest period of Hergé's life and career was about to begin.

At first, like many Belgians, Hergé and his wife fled to France; they stayed near Paris in a house on loan from the famous French comic artist Marijac. But Hergé yearned to get back to his drawing table and envied the neutrality of the Swiss. When Belgian King Leopold III encouraged his subjects to return to work, Hergé moved back to Brussels. He was immediately hired by the major newspaper *Le Soir* – it was dubbed *Le Soir Volé*, the Stolen Evening Times, after the War. Because of *Tintin*'s fame, *Le Soir* decided to launch a children's supplement, *Le Soir Jeunesse*, that would feature the adventures of the intrepid reporter. On 17 October 1940, *Tintin* made his trumpeted return in an all-new story, *The Crab with the Golden Claws*. Later, paper shortages forced the cancellation of the children's supplement and *Tintin* became a regular daily strip in *Le Soir*.

During the war, Hergé's attitude can best be summarised as follows: he tried to remain neutral as best he could. But to be neutral in times like those, living inside an occupied country, was not an easy task. And where is the line that separates neutrality from complicity?

Before the war, Hergé had denounced fascism in *King Ottokar's Sceptre*. In 1940 he spurned advances from the pro-Nazi Belgian royalists known as 'Rexists.' Two of his books were forbidden by the Nazis: *Tintin In America* and *The Black Island*. His brother, Paul, was a lieutenant in the Belgian army, a member of the resistance who continued to fight and was later wanted by the Germans. In 1943, Hergé was questioned by the

Gestapo about his relations with his brother.

On the other hand, Hergé came from a conservative Catholic background, whose values included decency and honesty, but which also had an ugly side that easily led or misled some to fascism. His 1941 story, *The Shooting Star*, sadly echoed the anti-Semitic prejudices of the times and consciously or unconsciously gave all the good roles to the pro-Axis and neutral states, while making America into a villain.

While working for *Le Soir*, Hergé also became friends with other writers and artists; some were not as neutral as he was and others may have been unfairly tarred with the same brush. In any event, there was also guilt by association. These ambiguities were common to virtually everyone living and working in Belgium or in France at the time – but not everyone was *Tintin*'s father...

In September 1944, when Belgium was liberated, the entire editorial team of *Le Soir*, which technically included Hergé, were fired and investigated. Some fled, others were jailed, lost their licenses or their civic rights. His former editor, Abbott Wallez, his friend and co-writer, Jacques Van Melkebeke, and several other of his relations suddenly found themselves on a new blacklist – or worse. Hergé himself was arrested and questioned several times, although never charged with anything.

In 1942 paper shortages had convinced Casterman to ask Hergé to reformat and colour his earlier works. He worked alone with Alice Devos, so at the beginning of 1944 Hergé entrusted that task to Edgar P Jacobs, who later became a renowned comics artist with his *Blake & Mortimer* series. During this dark time, Hergé retreated from the public eye, concentrating on the republication programme, grimly contemplating the end of *Tintin*, and even emigration to South America.

Rescue came in the person of publisher Raymond Leblanc who, in late 1945, met with Hergé and offered to launch a weekly children's magazine to compete with the better-known *Spirou* and *Bravo*; that magazine was to be entitled *Le Journal de Tintin*. Leblanc had been a resistance fighter and his war credentials were impeccable. Although that was not enough to protect *Tintin*'s first editor, Jacques Van Melkebeke, who had to be let go, it was enough to give Hergé – and *Tintin* – a new lease of life.

Le Journal de Tintin was launched on 26 September 1946 and became a success with a French edition and a cumulative printrun of nearly 100,000 copies. It also helped boost the sales of the *Tintin* books. For the first time, these reached the 100,000 mark for a newly-released title.

By the early 1950s, the 'silver age' of *Tintin* was in full bloom with classics like *Explorers on the Moon*. In 1950, Hergé created the Studios Hergé to assist him in what had become a real enterprise. Other renowned artists, such as Bob De Moor, Jacques Martin (creator of *Alix*) and Roger Leloup (creator of *Yoko Tsuno*), joined his staff. *Popol & Virginie* was reformatted, recoloured and published in 1952, and with the help of Jacques Martin, a final episode of *Jo, Zette & Jocko*, abandoned before the War, was completed and published in 1954.

Hergé's physical and mental health, however, suffered from the additional demands and pressures put upon him, and twice he was forced to stop work on *Tintin*. Then on 17 February 1952, he and his wife were involved in a car accident.

In 1956, Hergé began a secret relationship with 22-year-old colourist, Fanny Vlamynck, who had been hired by his Studios in 1952. As the popularity of *Tintin* reached new heights with the television cartoon series produced by Raymond Leblanc's studio Belvision in 1956 and 1957, Hergé's mood became darker. He became estranged from his wife, underwent Jungian psychoanalysis and sought spiritual guidance. This tumultuous period produced his best and most personal Tintin book, *Tintin In Tibet*.

In 1960, Hergé left Germaine and moved in with Fanny. He married her in 1977. Meanwhile, *Tintin*'s popularity grew by leaps and bounds. Two live action films were produced. French President Général de Gaulle called the character "his only international rival." Initial book sales for a new title reached the million mark in 1969.

Yet, Hergé appeared to have turned a page on that part of his life, as he had on his first marriage. The production of new books began to slow down and with *The Castafiore Emerald*, published in 1962, he began deconstructing *Tintin*. In 1965, he withdrew from *Le Journal de Tintin* which, under the editorship of Michel Greg, was evolving into a more modern product. Hergé was moving on.

He became interested in modern art and travelled

around the world with Fanny, most notably to the United States in 1971 and to Taiwan in 1973. His interest in Oriental philosophies grew. He started receiving awards and honours, and *Tintin* began to become the subject of exhibits. In 1976, Hergé was miraculously able to renew his relationship with Tchang Tchong-Jen, first by letters, then in person when the Chinese sculptor was allowed to travel to Europe in the spring of 1981.

In the meantime, Hergé's health had taken a turn for the worse. In 1979, during the celebration of *Tintin's* 50th Anniversary, he seemed very tired and anaemic. Soon after, he was diagnosed with a form of bone disease and leukaemia, requiring weekly blood transfusions.

Hergé was finally hospitalised on 25 February 1983 and died on 3 March.

Exeunt

Hergé's death made his wife, Fanny, the sole heir and controller of the *Tintin* business.

The day-to-day management of the Studios Hergé continued to be handled by Alain Baran, who had been hired as Hergé's personal secretary in 1978 and had been promoted to manager in 1981. The major two issues to be dealt with were the completion of *Tintin and Alph-Art*, the last book left unfinished by Hergé, and a live action film project by Steven Spielberg, who had contacted Hergé in November 1982, and had visited Fanny and the Studios soon after his death. The project did not take off and the rights reverted in 1988.

Ultimately, Fanny Rémi took the decision not to complete *Tintin and Alph-Art* but to publish it unfinished, and to close the Studios Hergé at the end of 1986, replacing them with various business entities, including a Hergé Foundation.

In 1988, Raymond Leblanc decided to sell *Le Journal de Tintin*, which stopped publication in November, and was replaced by a new magazine called *Tintin Reporter*, published with the financial support of a Catholic French financial group. However, the title never became profitable and was cancelled seven months later. During that time, a contract for a new animated television series adapting all of the books (except for the first two) was signed with animation partners Ellipse, a division of powerful media group Canal+, and Canadian studio Nelvana.

However, in 1990, Fanny Rémi decided to break with Alain Baran. A new business structure called Moulinsart was created and its management entrusted to Nick Rodwell, a young British man who had discovered *Tintin* through the 1957 animated television series. Rodwell had appeared on the scene in 1983 as a potential licensing agent for the United Kingdom. He later joined the management team, and was particularly involved in foreign licensing. He and Baran had not seen eye-to-eye on the direction the business should take.

Rodwell eventually married Fanny Rémi in 1994. His strategy since has relied on reducing the number of licences to better monitor the image and quality of the

Tintin brand. Moulinsart bought back the merchandising rights from Canal+ and increased its control over the use of *Tintin* images.

In 2002, Spielberg's new studio, DreamWorks, reoptioned the rights to *Tintin*. Five years later, Spielberg announced that he had teamed up with Peter Jackson, the director of *The Lord of the Rings* trilogy, to coproduce and direct a film based on *Secret of the Unicorn* and Red Rackham's *Treasure*, using the motion capture technology developed by Jackson's New Zealand-based Weta Digital studio.

After some financing delays, the film was shot in early 2009, then sent to Weta for processing. *The Adventures of Tintin: Secret of the Unicorn* was released in 2011, after having its premiere in Brussels. Peter Jackson is scheduled to direct the sequel, based on *The Seven Crystal Balls* and *Prisoners of the Sun*.

Before Tintin

Before there was Hergé there was Georges Rémi, and before there was Tintin there was Totor. Whatever similarities existed between Tintin and Hergé, there were even more between Georges Rémi aka Curious Fox, Scout Leader of the Squirrel Troop, and Totor, Scout Leader of the Beetle Troop.

Les Aventures de Totor, Chef de Patrouille des Hannetons (*The Adventures of Totor, Scout Leader of the Beetle Troop*) made its first appearance in *Le Boy-Scout Belge* in July 1926, and continued for 26 pages, until July 1929, when Rémi decided to devote himself entirely to *Tintin*, which he had created six months before for *Le Petit Vingtième*.

The *Totor* adventures came in the form of four, then six, then eight square panels to a page. Harking back to an earlier form of comics, the narrative text was typeset under the panels, with word balloons being used very rarely and only for exclamations (e.g.: 'Hands up!' '?' '!' 'Aie!').

Graphically, Totor was virtually identical to Tintin in every respect, except for his scout uniform. Hergé later acknowledged that his early work was much influenced by that of French comics artist Alain Saint-Ogan

(1895–1974), who had just created an adventure series entitled *Zig et Puce* for the French magazine *Le Dimanche Illustré* (*The Sunday Illustrated*) starting in May 1925. (While working on *Tintin in the Congo*, Hergé met Saint-Ogan, who encouraged him in his efforts and gave him a signed original page of art.)

Zig et Puce was the first modern French comics series, reflecting and incorporating not only the influences of earlier comics, such as Louis Forton's seminal *Les Pieds Nickelés* (which also had narrative text typeset under the panel art) but also of American cartoonists. Two such foreign influences were George McManus' *Bringing Up Father* and Martin Branner's *Winnie Winkle*, which were both published with enormous success in France at the time.

In addition to Alain Saint-Ogan's influence, Hergé also credited Léon Degrelle, the then American correspondent of *Le Vingtième Siècle*, who sent copies of US newspapers to Belgium, for introducing him to the American artists' sense of composition and storytelling. Indeed, as one reads through the last pages of *Totor* and the first pages of the first *Tintin* story, *Tintin In the Land of the Soviets*, which were created simultaneously, one is struck by Hergé's rapid progress in mastering the rules of the medium, and how quickly his work evolved from static illustrations to incorporating action and dynamic composition.

Zig et Puce was the first French comic to use word balloons exclusively; it was drawn in a clear, semi-caricature line, contrasting cartoony heroes against semi-realistic backgrounds, owing much to the wood-engraving type of illustrations popular in newspapers and magazines at the time. *Zig et Puce* also established most of the modern comics storytelling conventions.

In their first adventure, entitled *En Route Towards America*, two teenage boys, Zig and Puce, are side-tracked to Africa, travel to the North Pole in a balloon, collect a pet penguin they christen Alfred, reach Japan by submarine and, eventually, New York by plane.

Both graphically and story-wise, Hergé followed the *Zig et Puce* model: Totor, too, like Tintin soon after, embarked on a steamship to go to America, in his case to be with his uncle Pad Hatt, a big Texas rancher. The New York which Totor visited was unreal, owing more to the unbridled imagination of a young European artist than to any real-life documentation. Totor unwittingly captured gangster John Blood before moving on to a series of western adventures. Totor rescued his family from hostile Indians and from the dreaded outlaw Jim Blackcat. On the last page, after rescuing his aunt, Totor returned to Europe to a triumphant scout reception, probably justified by his gift to the movement of a chest of jewels he had found along the way!

Unlike the more steady *Zig et Puce*, however, *Totor* was told in a serial style, with cliffhangers at the end of every page. Also, what was unusual if not ground-breaking for the times, was that the narration under the panels provided a tongue-in-cheek counterpoint to the earnest action depicted in the art. Indeed, the entire series was presented as the work of the fictional United Rovers Film Company! In the later instalments, the credits even read 'Hergé Moving Pictures!'

Everything that made *Tintin* what it later became was seminally present in *Totor*: the appealing charm of the art, deceptively simple yet sophisticated; the break-neck pace of the story where, not unlike cliffhanger serials, one never knew what might happen next, yet counterpointed with humour, thereby introducing a reflective distance between the narrative and the reader; and finally, the ambition of the artist to tell stories which are like motion pictures, pretending with cheek that they are, yet simultaneously admitting that they are not.

Totor reads as if an adult was retelling one of those early American western serials, whose popularity had exploded in Europe, to a group of children. On the one hand he is exciting the children, but on the other he is winking at the adults as if to say, 'you and I know that this is not serious.'

Beyond comics and film influences, much has been written about Hergé's other sources of inspiration for *Tintin*, real or imagined, conscious or unconscious – an artist is after all the product of what he reads and sees.

Certainly, the tradition of extraordinary, globe-trot-ting adventures, which was started by French writer Jules Verne (1828–1905) in his *Voyages Extraordinaires* (*Extraordinary Voyages*) imprint, was very much alive in the young-adult fiction of the times.

By the 1920s, many of Verne's themes and stories had been popularised in other media – such as the early pictures of filmmaker Georges Méliès (1861–1938) – and had given rise to an entire school of French popular authors including André Laurie, Louis Boussenard, Georges Le Faure, Gustave Le Rouge, Paul d'Ivoi etc.

Adventure magazines were filled with what we might label 'Proto-Tintins' – fearless teenagers or young reporters, embarking on extraordinary adventures around the world, making full use of then exotic means of travel such as aeroplanes and submarines.

For example, Marcel Priollet, writing under the pseudonym of R–M Nizerolles, created the character of a young, heroic Parisian kid named Tintin for his pulp series *Les Voyages Aériens d'Un Petit Parisien à Travers le Monde* (*The Aerial Voyages of a Little Parisian Around the World*), serialised in 111 issues (382 chapters, 11,776 pages), published by Ferenczi in 1910. In it, the indomitable Tintin had various adventures, first around the world, both in the skies and underground, then later across the solar system.

Two other notorious 'Proto-Tintins' may also have influenced Hergé's creation – if only because of their popularity: Lavarède, the creation of writer Paul d'Ivoi (Paul-Charles Deleutre, 1856–1915), was a young man who embarked on a trip around the world with only five pennies in his pocket in *Les Cinq Sous de Lavarède* (1894), and Rouletabille, the creation of writer Gaston Leroux (1868–1927, better known for *Phantom of the Opera*), was a young, fearless crime-solving reporter who travelled to Russia in *Rouletabille Chez le Tsar* (1913).

The Books

Tintin In the Land of the Soviets

Publishing History:
1. Serialisation in Belgium in *Le Petit Vingtième* from 10 January 1929, and in France in *Coeurs Vaillants* from 26 October 1930.
2. *Les Aventures de Tintin, Reporter du Petit Vingtième au Pays des Soviets*, 138 pages, black & white, Editions du Petit Vingtième, Brussels, 1930.
3. *Les Aventures de Tintin au Pays des Soviets*, limited edition (500), Studio Hergé, Brussels, 1969.
4. In *Archives Hergé*, Volume 1, Editions Casterman, Tournai, 1973.
5. *Les Aventures de Tintin, Reporter du Petit Vingtième au Pays des Soviets*, facsimile edition of 2, Editions Casterman, Tournai, 1981.

At the end of 1928, Abbott Norbert Wallez, the editor of the Belgian Catholic newspaper *Le Vingtième Siècle*, asked Georges Rémi to edit a weekly children's supplement entitled *Le Petit Vingtième*. In issue 11, on 10 January 1929, Hergé launched *Tintin In the Land of the Soviets*, published in weekly, two-page instalments.

At first a remake of *Totor* – a 'Totor goes East' – the series gained in style and power as Hergé mastered his craft. It was so successful that, towards the end of its run, *Le Vingtième Siècle* was able to print six times as many copies on the day of the week the *Tintin* strip ran.

Later, the French Catholic magazine *Coeurs Vaillants* (*Brave Hearts*) began serialising *Tintin* in France; in Belgium, a hardcover collection of the series was published by *Le Vingtième Siècle*. The first 500 copies (out of a printrun of 5,000) were numbered, and are today valued at over £10,000. Strangely, a page was missing in that edition – the page published in issue 60 of *Le Petit Vingtième*.

When Hergé began to redraw his earlier *Tintin* stories for the modernised colour versions produced at Casterman's suggestion, starting in 1942, he chose not to redraw *Tintin In the Land of the Soviets*. The reason given was that the story was too crude. It is also possible that the story was too virulently anti-Communist to be well received in the immediate post-war years, when most of Western Europe had substantial pro-Communist sympathies. And Hergé had learned to be careful of mixing politics and comics...

Because of the rarity of the original edition, pirated editions began to surface. In 1969, to celebrate *Tintin*'s 40th anniversary, Hergé released a 500-copy limited facsimile edition, which only served to increase the number of pirated editions. Hergé then authorised the reprinting of *Tintin In the Land of the Soviets* in the first omnibus volume of *Archives Hergé* (which also reprinted *Totor*, *Tintin In the Congo* and *Tintin In America*) in 1973. That did nothing to stop the flood of pirated editions. Eventually, a true facsimile edition was published in 1981.

Plot: Tintin, a young reporter for *Le Petit Vingtième*, and his fox terrier Milou (Snowy in English – the English name will now be used throughout) are sent to Moscow to report on the conditions of life in the Soviet Union. Tintin eventually reaches Moscow, in spite of the hurdles thrown in his path by the GPU. During his journey, he discovers the horrors of bolshevism: deserted factories, hunger, rigged elections etc. The GPU finally captures Tintin in Moscow. After a daring escape, he infiltrates the Red Army. Unmasked, he is forced to flee in the snowy waste. Eventually, he comes across what seems to be a haunted cabin, but turns out to be the secret entrance to underground vaults where Lenin, Trotsky and Stalin have hidden the plundered wealth of Russia. Thanks to Snowy, Tintin again escapes death, flees by plane and returns to a triumphant reception in Brussels.

Characters: Except for Tintin and Snowy, none of the characters have any personality; they serve as mere props in the unfolding story, being either evil Communists or oppressed Russians.

Continuity: None at this stage.

Influences: All experts agree that Hergé obtained his information about Russia solely from the 1928 book *Moscou Sans Voiles* (*Moscow Without Veils*) by Joseph Douillet, a former Belgian consul in Rostov. All of Tintin's daring escapes, using cars, planes and locomotives, are story devices commonly used in movie serials of the times. Even then, the 'haunted cabin' used as a decoy by the villains to protect their lair was a hoary plot twist. Finally, the daring western reporter travelling to Russia to expose Bolshevik crimes was standard fare for readers of popular weekly pulps such as the *Journal des Voyages* and *L'Intrépide* (*The Fearless*).

Trivia: For the first and only time in his career, Tintin is actually shown writing an article for his newspaper.

Review: Today, *Tintin In the Land of the Soviets* can only be considered in its historical context. Story-wise and graphically, Hergé was learning his craft before our eyes, improvising new story twists on a weekly basis, not proceeding along a carefully written plot planned in advance. When the story begins, Hergé is still in a 'proto-Tintin' phase: a two-dimensional hero with limited dialogue in simple situations. By the end of the book, Tintin has become the character we know today and Snowy has acquired his personality. The endearing dynamics between the young hero and his faithful, resourceful pet come across vividly and charmingly.

In terms of art, Hergé learned to move his camera, make his compositions more dynamic and experimented with his line. As the book progresses, he is not afraid to be daring in his choice of images, and some panels anticipate the minimalist achievements of what is now called the 'Clear Line' style. Rarely in the history of comics has one single book shown so much progress and evolution between its first and last page.

As to the political contents, they deserve to be evaluated taking into account what we have since learned about the Soviet Union. After World War Two, Hergé refused to redraw *Tintin In the Land of the Soviets* and preferred to let it remain out of print for decades. Maybe he was concerned about what he thought might be seen as a naïve, caricatured and bigoted attack on communism? Hergé was knowledgeable enough to realise that being labelled an 'anti-communiste primaire' (bigoted anti-Communist) would hurt his standing among the left-leaning intelligentsia of the times. Yet, with hindsight, *Tintin In the Land of the Soviets*, while as caricatured and poorly-researched as *Tintin In The Congo*, which Hergé redrew and reissued, has actually better withstood the test of time.

It may be argued that, just as Hergé was afraid of confronting the Nazi invaders during World War Two he was also afraid of confronting the European left of the 1950s and 1960s, and so he partially disowned *Tintin In the Land of the Soviets*, which he undoubtedly also saw as a rough, unpolished work, unworthy of its successors. However, like a nut, the outside may be a bit rough, but inside, the meat is still fresh. 1/5.

Tintin In the Congo

Publishing History:

1. Serialisation in Belgium in *Le Petit Vingtième* from 5 May 1930, and in France in *Coeurs Vaillants* from 20 March 1932.
2. *Les Aventures de Tintin, Reporter du Petit Vingtième Au Congo*, 115 pages, black & white, Editions du Petit Vingtième, Brussels, 1931.

3. *Tintin au Congo*, Editions Casterman, Tournai, 1937.
4. *Tintin au Congo*, 62 pages, colour, Editions Casterman, Tournai, 1946.
5. In *Archives Hergé*, Volume 1, Editions Casterman, Tournai, 1973.
6. *Les Aventures de Tintin, Reporter du Petit Vingtième Au Congo*, facsimile edition of 2, Editions Casterman, Tournai, 1982.

Since Totor had gone to America, Hergé wanted to send Tintin there too for his second adventure but Abbott Wallez asked him instead to send his hero to the Belgian Congo. The story of *Tintin In the Congo* was first serialised in weekly two-page instalments in *Le Petit Vingtième* from 5 May 1930 to 11 June 1931, and subsequently resold to the French magazine *Coeurs Vaillants*. Once again, a triumphant reception was staged at Brussels' train station on 9 July 1931 with a live boy impersonating Tintin to celebrate the hero's return.

The original book collection was published by *Le Petit Vingtième* as well but, in 1934, Hergé resold the book rights to Belgian publisher Casterman, who became his exclusive book publisher from then on. Casterman reissued the book in 1937.

After World War Two, Hergé totally redrew, reformatted and coloured *Tintin In the Congo*, shrinking it from its initial 110 three-strip pages to the new standard 62 four-strip page format suggested by Casterman in 1942. The dialogue was also improved, though many of Snowy's best lines were cut!

In the 1970s, responding to collectors' demand, the

original black & white version of *Tintin In the Congo*
was reprinted in the first volume of *Archives Hergé*. A
true facsimile of the original edition was published in
1982.

Plot: Tintin embarks for the Congo. During the
journey, Snowy uncovers a mysterious Stowaway, who
seems to be on a mission to stop Tintin. In the Congo,
Tintin hires Coco, a young native driver. Tintin
befriends the Babaoro'm tribe, but Muganga, their
witch doctor, becomes jealous of his popularity and
teams up with the Stowaway to frame Tintin. Thanks to
Coco, Tintin proves his innocence. The Stowaway and
Muganga then foment a war with a neighbouring tribe,
but Tintin uses an electro-magnet to impress them into
peace. The Stowaway tries again to kill Tintin and
Snowy but they are rescued by a kind Missionary.
Tintin eventually pursues the Stowaway, who dies
when he falls into a crocodile-infested river. Thanks to
a letter found on his body, Tintin meets Gibbons, a
gangster in the employ of Al Capone who wishes to
corner the diamond market. Afraid of Tintin, Capone
ordered that he be eliminated. Tintin delivers the gangsters to the Belgian police. Then he returns to filming
and hunting wildlife and is eventually picked up by two
aviators who tell him he is wanted back in Belgium.

Characters: The only good guys are the devoted Coco,
who disappears halfway through the book, and the brave
Missionary Priest, who embodies all the virtues that the
editors of *Le Petit Vingtième* could wish for. The villains
are only marginally more interesting than those in
Tintin In the Land of the Soviets. The bearded Stowaway

is memorable only because of his sheer relentlessness in trying to kill Tintin. Muganga, the witch doctor, is more comic relief than threat. Gibbons and the other gangsters are disposed of in two pages – clearly, Hergé was using them purely to set up the theme of the next book, itching to deal with America.

Curiously, the opening pages in which Snowy comes to blows with an annoying parrot anticipate numerous future scenes in which Hergé depicted irritating parrots, bent on causing as much humorous havoc as possible.

Continuity: Tintin's trip to the Soviet Union is referred to several times. Al Capone does not appear, but is introduced. Panel 1 of page 1 of the redrawn 1946 version retroactively includes a shot of Thomson and Thompson, as yet unidentified.

Influences: Tintin In the Congo owes its entire existence – with the exception of the clichéd element of the diamond traffickers, probably borrowed from *Jungle Jim*-type serials – to the Belgian Missionaries' literature of the times. No doubt it was torn directly from the pages of *Le Vingtième Siècle*, for which the spread of Christianity and the civilising mission of the West in Africa were axioms of faith.

Trivia: In panel 1 of page 1, the crowd wishing Tintin goodbye includes Hergé's other comics heroes, street urchins Quick and Flupke. In the redrawn 1946 version, the same panel additionally includes caricatures of Hergé himself, his then assistant, Edgar P Jacobs and his friend Jacques Van Melkebeke among the journalists.

When *Tintin In the Congo* was first published in Scandinavia, page 56, in which Tintin blows up a rhinoceros, was deemed too unbelievable, and was redrawn to show the hero falling asleep while a curious rhino causes his gun to discharge by mistake. Also, boa constrictors, like the one that threatens to eat Snowy, don't exist in Africa.

Review: It is hard to justify *Tintin In the Congo* on almost any level. Graphically, the book is in the continuity of *Tintin In the Land of the Soviets*, and contains little stylistic changes or evolution. Either Hergé thought that the Congo was a well-manicured place, or drawing a real jungle was beyond his abilities, but in any event, the visual representation of Africa is flat and uninspired. It seems that Hergé is marking time until he can sink his teeth into something more exciting.

The same is true of the story. In spite of its numerous cliffhangers, the book appears listless, as if Hergé's heart was not truly into it. The manic energy of *Tintin In the Land of the Soviets* is gone; *Tintin In the Congo* reads like a bad travelogue with perfunctory perils to keep the reader's attention. There is more emotion in an early scene where Tintin rescues Snowy from drowning in shark-infested waters than in the entire rest of the story.

It is a given that *Tintin In the Congo* is pure Missionary propaganda, but did all of the Africans need to be uniformly depicted as children, easily fooled, aping European fashions, superstitious and scared of their own shadows? Tintin is the Great White Hope, virtually a god by the end of the book, which shows

Tintin-shaped idols being worshipped in a village. In the original black & white version, Tintin is shown teaching African children that their motherland is Belgium. In the redrawn 1946 version, Hergé, in a half-hearted effort to make the book seem less foolish, changed the scene into an elementary math lesson. But in the end, there is nothing that he could do to plaster over its inherently ludicrous, if well-meaning, nature.

The wildlife is treated in the same fashion: like all great white hunters Tintin slaughters antelopes, apes and elephants with abandon – except for one instance where he disguises himself to film some giraffes.

Tintin In the Land of the Soviets was no real-life documentary, but at least it bore some relevance to the reality of Russian life. *Tintin In the Congo* has none – it is ultimately not about Africa in the 1930s, but about how Belgian Catholics saw Africa in the 1930s. Not a pretty sight. 0/5.

Tintin In America

Publishing History:

1. Serialisation in Belgium in *Le Petit Vingtième* from 3 September 1931, and in France in *Coeurs Vaillants* from 2 April 1933.

2. *Les Aventures de Tintin, Reporter du Petit Vingtième En Amérique*, 123 pages, black & white, Editions du Petit Vingtième, Brussels, 1932.

3. *Les Aventures de Tintin et Milou en Amérique*, smaller size, rewritten, Editions Ogéo-Coeurs Vaillants, Paris, 1934.

4. *Tintin en Amérique*, Editions Casterman, Tournai, 1934.
5. *Tintin en Amérique*, 62 pages, colour, Editions Casterman, Tournai, 1945.
6. In *Archives Hergé*, Volume 1, Editions Casterman, Tournai, 1973.
7. *Les Aventures de Tintin, Reporter du Petit Vingtième En Amérique*, facsimile edition of 2, Editions Casterman, Tournai, 1983.

Tintin In America, initially entitled *Les Aventures de Tintin, Reporter à Chicago* (*The Adventures of Tintin, Reporter In Chicago*), began serialisation in *Le Petit Vingtième* in September 1931 and ran for about a year.

The first hardcover collection was published by *Le Petit Vingtième* and was reprinted by Casterman in 1934, when Hergé sold them the book rights. *Tintin In America* was, in fact, the first *Tintin* book they published. There was a short-lived, rare, smaller size, earlier French edition published with the magazine *Coeurs Vaillants*.

Tintin In America was reformatted and coloured by Hergé in 1945; the original edition was eventually reprinted in the first volume of *Archives Hergé* in 1973. A true facsimile of the original edition was published in 1983.

Plot: Tintin arrives in Chicago. He is kidnapped by Al Capone, whom he eventually captures. Tintin then fights gangster Bobby Smiles, surviving assassination attempts and foiling a truck hijacking. Smiles flees to the Far West and sets a tribe of Indians against Tintin.

Tintin continues to pursue Smiles, escapes being lynched by mistake and finally captures Smiles in his mountain hideout. Tintin is now a celebrity. Snowy is kidnapped. Tintin manages to find the kidnappers' lair and frees Snowy, but the ringleader gets away. Later, Tintin captures him and the boss of an automated corned-beef factory who tried to kill him. During a ceremonial dinner, the Crime Syndicate abducts Tintin and attempts to drown him in Lake Michigan, but he escapes again. Tintin's actions result in the arrest of 335 gangsters and he is given a triumphant ticker-tape parade before he returns to Europe.

Characters: The best villain in the book is the deceptively amiable Bobby Smiles, much better than Al Capone, who is disposed of in a few pages. The unnamed ringleader of the kidnappers' gang and the leader of the Crime Syndicate don't measure up to the affable, yet deadly, Smiles. He is the first great villain in the *Tintin* series. The incompetent hotel detective, MacAdam, anticipates the antics of the Thompsons, and the comical, drunken sheriff who fails to prevent Tintin's near-lynching anticipates Captain Haddock.

Continuity: We meet Al Capone, who was mentioned in *Tintin In the Congo*.

Influences: This is the America that Hergé wanted to portray in *Totor* but had not: from the skyscrapers and crime-infested streets of Chicago to the vistas of the Far West. Hergé relishes putting Tintin through all of the classic scenes from the serials: the lynching, being tied to rail tracks, being captured by Indians etc. Tintin's sharpshooting prowess in the arrest of Bobby Smiles is straight out of the *Buffalo Bill* serials, and the skulduggery of the gangsters taking the hero 'for a drive' out of *Little Caesar*. Even though Hergé researched by reading magazines and a book about Indians, *L'Histoire des Peaux-Rouges* (*The History of the Redskins*) by Paul Coze, this is not the real America but the mythic version presented on the silver screen and in the literary serials of Gustave Le Rouge and others.

Trivia: Al Capone is the only real-life figure to ever have starred in a *Tintin* story. In the original black & white edition, Hergé never showed his face, which was kept hidden under a scarf. By 1945, perhaps because Capone was no longer a real concern, Hergé removed the scarf and drew the notorious scarred face.

Other changes made between the original black & white edition and the 1945 version included deleting Mary Pickford from Tintin's ceremonial dinner, and removing two fiendish, dog-eating Chinese hoodlums. By then, Hergé knew better. The name of the Indian tribe was also changed from the farcical Orteils Ficelés (Tied Toes) to the more realistic Pieds Noirs (Black Feet).

Review: With *Tintin In America*, Hergé made another leap forward. While the story still rambles on without a unifying thread and follows an 'everything but the kitchen sink' approach, it is nevertheless more tightly plotted than its predecessors. Hergé succeeds in embracing all of the classic American myths in a narrative that withstands comparison with the vision of America depicted in other literary serials of the times, such as Le Rouge & Guitton's *La Conspiration des Milliardaires* (*The Billionaires' Conspiracy*, 1900). *Tintin In America* may be naïve and oversimplified due to lack of first-hand knowledge, but it is never condescending.

Hergé's remarkably concise, yet effective, demonstration of how American natives were exploited was an astonishing piece of narrative. After Tintin finds an oil well, he is plagued by businessmen who believe the well belongs to him, and bid up to $100,000 for it. After he tells them the land belongs to the Indians, the businessmen offer the Natives $25 and tell them they have half-an-hour to pack. The next panel shows them being driven away at bayonet's point by the army. Two panels later, a thriving business centre is already built and operating. Reportedly, this bit of social satire was unpopular with some foreign publishers, but Hergé always resisted pressures to change it.

Graphically, the art and the storytelling also show marked progress. Some scenes, such as the night scenes near Lake Michigan, or the horse pursuit of Bobby Smiles, are superbly drawn, with the clarity that makes the Clear Line style so successful. For the first time in the series, some panels can be taken out of the story and looked at as individual pieces of art.

One of the full-page colour illustrations drawn for *Le Petit Vingtième* (not reprinted in the graphic novels) shows Tintin standing, gun in hand, on the running board of a speeding car, chasing gangsters in a teeming American metropolis. The image is eerily reminiscent of a famous original *Doc Savage* cover. This shows how well, even at a distance, Hergé captured the spirit of

America. The covers drawn by Hergé for the earlier editions of *Tintin In America* emphasised Tintin as a cowboy. The later image, a redrawn version of a *Petit Vingtième* full-page colour illustration, gives the spotlight to a finely drawn Indian chief, with Tintin nervously awaiting his fate tied to a post in the background. It is a stunning image.

Tintin In America is still a work of transition, but it is the first *Tintin* book that Hergé felt completely comfortable offering to the world, the first that he licensed outside of *Le Petit Vingtième* and later redrew, and the first with that intangible epic quality that characterises the *Tintin* saga. 2/5

Cigars of the Pharaoh

Publishing History:

1. Serialisation in Belgium in *Le Petit Vingtième* from 8 December 1932, and in France in *Coeurs Vaillants* from 16 September 1934.

2. *Les Aventures de Tintin, Reporter en Orient – Les Cigares du Pharaon*, 127 pages, black & white, Editions Casterman, Tournai, 1934.

3. *Les Cigares du Pharaon*, 62 pages, colour, Editions Casterman, Tournai, 1955.

4. In *Archives Hergé*, Volume 2, Editions Casterman, Tournai, 1979.

5. *Les Aventures de Tintin, Reporter en Orient – Les Cigares du Pharaon*, facsimile edition of 2, Editions Casterman, Tournai, 1983.

Cigars of the Pharaoh, initially entitled *Tintin en Orient* (*Tintin In the Orient*), began serialisation in *Le Petit Vingtième* in December 1932. The first hardcover collection was directly published by Casterman, under the new licensing agreement signed by Hergé in 1934.

Cigars of the Pharaoh was reformatted and coloured by Hergé only in 1955, the last of all the earlier books – for the most part because of the popularity of the black & white edition. The original edition was eventually reprinted in the second omnibus volume of *Archives Hergé* in 1973. A true facsimile of the original edition was published in 1983.

Plot: Tintin meets eccentric Egyptologist Philémon Siclone (Sophocles Sarcophagus) and film mogul Rastapopoulos. He is then framed for possession of cocaine and arrested by two inept policemen, Thomson and Thompson. He escapes and joins Sarcophagus on an expedition to locate the tomb of pharaoh Kih-Oskh. Inside, Tintin finds boxes of cigars. He and Sarcophagus are gassed, thrown into sarcophagi and taken to Allan Thompson's ship (simply 'Allan' in the English version). To avoid the coastguard, Allan throws them into the sea. Tintin is rescued by a sailboat which, he later discovers, belongs to gun-runners. With the Thompsons on his trail, Tintin continues his journey, meeting friendly Sheikh Patrash Pasha and Rastapopoulos again. He is drafted in the local army and discovers that its Colonel is a member of the Kih-Oskh conspiracy. Tintin is arrested, then rescued by the Thompsons. He escapes in a plane, but is shot down over the Indian jungle. There he meets Sarcophagus, now insane, having been poisoned with Rajaijah (Rajajajah). Tintin confronts a Fakir with hypnotic powers, who has him locked up in an asylum. Eventually, Tintin escapes and meets the Maharajah of Rawhajpoutalah (Gaipajma), whose anti-opium policies make him an enemy of the conspiracy. Tintin sets a trap and follows the Fakir to an underground lair where the conspirators meet. Tintin captures the villains before being unmasked, but the Fakir escapes. He and the mysterious conspiracy leader kidnap the Maharajah's son. Tintin pursues them in a sports car. A rock slide renders the Fakir unconscious. The leader falls into a chasm. Tintin returns to a triumphant welcome in Gaipajma, where he finally discovers that the cigars were used as an opium smuggling device.

Characters: Cigars of the Pharaoh introduces a number of major recurring characters to the Tintin saga. The most important are undoubtedly the two inept detectives, initially called Agents X33 and X33b in the black & white version, then Durant and Durand in the stage plays written by Hergé in 1941 in collaboration with his friend, Jacques Van Melkebeke, and finally Dupond and Dupont. (Dupont with a 't' is the one with the pointy moustache.) They are, of course, Thompson and Thomson in the English editions. The Thompsons' limited intelligence, their discombobulated way of expressing themselves – one usually repeating and garbling what the other said by adding 'to be precise' – make them ideal foils and comic relief. Like Peter Sellers' Clouseau, the Thompsons are living caricatures, and invariably look at other cultures as caricatures as well – not unlike what Hergé himself had done up to that point.

The other character of note is Rastapopoulos, Tintin's future arch-enemy, whose identity as the mysterious leader of the Kih-Oskh conspiracy is not exposed until the next book. The notion of a flamboyant movie mogul being the secret head of a criminal empire has lost none of its immediacy. Other recurring supporting characters also include the mercenary Captain Allan, one of Rastapopoulos' henchmen, the endearing Portuguese merchant, Oliveira da Figueira, a prodigious salesman who could sell anything to anyone, and Arab Sheikh Patrash Pasha.

Continuity: Cigars of the Pharaoh is the first part of the *Tintin In the Orient* arc, which continues in *The Blue Lotus*. In addition to Rastapopoulos and Allan Thompson, some of the Arabic characters and themes are revisited in *Land of Black Gold*.

Influences: The earlier portion of the book, dealing with the search for the lost tomb of Kih-Oskh, and the discovery of the mummified Egyptologists therein, was inspired by the famous discovery of King Tut's tomb by Howard Carter in 1922, and its ensuing tragic events. Hergé revisited that theme, in a far more dramatic fashion, in *The Seven Crystal Balls*.

Like its predecessors, the story incorporates an odd mixture of clichéd movie plots. Yet Hergé is able to show a degree of self-awareness by introducing a scene in which Arab villains whipping a helpless blonde white girl are revealed to be part of a clichéd Hollywood film!

The international drug ring, the Red Sea gun-runners, the stormy night at the bungalow, the cursed dagger and, finally, the revelation of a secret sect of cowled villains dressed in robes bearing the mysterious Sign of Kih-Oskh are all elements torn from the pages of the adventure pulps of the times, such as Gustave Le Rouge's *Le Mystérieux Docteur Cornelius* (*The Mysterious Dr Cornelius*, 1912), with its Red Hand secret society, and Ponson du Terrail's sprawling saga of *Rocambole* (1860s), with its deadly Thugee conspiracies.

More original was the notion of Tintin being hunted by the police, framed for a crime he did not commit and ultimately trapped in a lunatic asylum – a nightmarish situation. These are Hitchcockian devices predating the works of the great filmmaker, and akin to Jean Valjean's flight in Victor Hugo's *Les Misérables* (1860), and the novels of John Buchan, which inspired Hitchcock, such as *The Thirty-Nine Steps* (1915) and *Greenmantle* (1916).

Trivia: When Patrash Pasha tells Tintin that he is a fan of his adventures, in the original black & white edition, he proudly shows him a copy of *Tintin In America*. In the first colour edition, the book was replaced by *Tintin In the Congo*. In later editions, it was replaced by *Destination Moon*, an odd choice since that book takes place almost twenty years later.

When Tintin discovers the conspiracy's underground lair in Gaipajma, in the black & white edition, he first comes across a perilous chamber filled with cobras, which he distracts by throwing them a chocolate bar. That scene was removed in the revised, coloured edition.

JEAN-MARC AND RANDY LOFFICIER

The gun-running captain who rescues Tintin in the
Red Sea is patterned after Henri de Monfreid
(1879–1974), a notorious Red Sea freebooter and
writer.

One of the mummified scientists in Kih-Oskh's
tomb is, again, a caricature of Hergé's colleague, Edgar
P Jacobs.

Review: Graphically, *Cigars of the Pharaoh* is on a
plateau between *Tintin In America* and Hergé's next leap
forward in *The Blue Lotus*. Hergé is expanding his visual
vocabulary and the book is filled with unforgettable
moments: the exploration of the tomb of Kih-Oskh
features the first dream sequence of the saga – there will
be others, each even stranger and more surreal; Tintin
lost at sea in a sarcophagus; the trek through the desert;
bathing and conversing with elephants; and finally, the
dramatic scenes in the villains' underground lair.

Hergé is still making it up as he goes, but he has
added two new ingredients to his formula: mystery and
fantasy. The story reads like a surreal thriller, drenched
with atmosphere, and evokes in the reader a sense of
dreamlike suspension of disbelief. Madness is not only
part of the plot of the book, it *is* the book. In *Cigars of
the Pharaoh*, the reader cannot tell the rational from the
insane. Sophocles Sarcophagus is already half-mad
when he is introduced. Later, Tintin has visions of
Egyptian gods. He converses with elephants through
music. He meets a fakir who can cloud men's minds
and perform the famous rope trick. At night, terror
stalks the land, as poisoned arrows shot through
windows cause their victims to lose their mind. Tragedy

strikes. Dark forces lurk at every turn. Even mild-mannered supporting characters are revealed to be members of a sinister conspiracy. Trust no one. At the centre of all that mayhem, there is the Tao-like Sign of Kih-Oskh, which shows up throughout the book, like the visual equivalent of a recurring musical theme, adding a note of pure oneirism. 3/5

The Blue Lotus

Publishing History:
1. Serialisation in Belgium in *Le Petit Vingtième* from 9 August 1934, and in France in *Coeurs Vaillants* from 29 December 1935.
2. *Les Aventures de Tintin Reporter en Extrême-Orient – Le Lotus Bleu*, 132 pages, black & white, Editions Casterman, Tournai, 1936.
3. *Le Lotus Bleu*, 62 pages, colour, Editions Casterman, Tournai, 1946.
4. In *Archives Hergé*, Volume 2, Editions Casterman, Tournai, 1979.
5. *Les Aventures de Tintin Reporter en Extrême-Orient – Le Lotus Bleu*, facsimile edition of 2, Editions Casterman, Tournai, 1985.

The Blue Lotus, initially entitled *Tintin en Extrême-Orient* (*Tintin In the Far East*), began serialisation in *Le Petit Vingtième* in August 1934. The first hardcover collection was published by Casterman in 1936.

After the publication of *Cigars of the Pharaoh*, Hergé was contacted by Father Gosset, chaplain of the

Chinese students attending the University of Louvain. Father Gosset suggested that Hergé obtain more accurate information about China in preparation for his next book. Hergé wholeheartedly agreed, and Father Gosset put him in touch with Tchang Tchong-Jen[1] (or Chang Chon-Chen), a Chinese student at the Fine Arts Academy of Brussels. Tchang not only helped Hergé with his research, but actually drew the Chinese ideograms used in the original version of the story.

The Blue Lotus was reformatted and coloured by Hergé in 1946. The original edition was reprinted in the second omnibus volume of *Archives Hergé* in 1973. A true facsimile of the original edition was published in 1985.

Plot: In Gaipajma, Tintin meets a Chinese man who only has time to utter 'Mitsuhirato' before being struck insane by Rajajajah. Tintin travels to Shanghai and

[1] Tchang Tchong-Jen (1905–1998) was Roman Catholic-educated and had decorated movie sets before winning a scholarship to study sculpture in 1931 at the Royal Academy of Fine Arts in Brussels. There, he became the man who taught Hergé about the realities of a China oppressed by foreign powers in the 1930s, and one of *Tintin*'s most beloved fictional characters. After his return to China in 1935 – before *The Blue Lotus* was published – Tchang went on to become an influential artist/sculptor and eventually the head of the Fine Arts Academy of Shanghai. Chang and Hergé were miraculously reunited in 1976, first through correspondence, then in person in 1981 in Brussels, two years before Hergé's death. In 1985, Chang and his daughter settled in France at the invitation of French Culture Minister, Jack Lang. Chang died on 8 October 1998 at age 93 of complications from a cold at the Maison des Artistes in Nogent-sur-Marne, outside Paris.

meets with Mitsuhirato, a Japanese who urges him to return to India. Thanks to Didi, a Chinese man who watches over him, he escapes two assassination attempts. Tintin eventually meets Didi, but too late – he has been struck by Rajajajah. Tintin leaves Shanghai but is kidnapped by the Sons of the Dragon, a Chinese society which fights opium and the Japanese, whose agent is Mitsuhirato. Their leader is Wang Jen-Ghie (Wang Chen-Yee), Didi's father. Tintin agrees to help; a radio intercept leads him to the Blue Lotus, an opium smoking den. He follows Mitsuhirato as he blows up a railroad. The Japanese use the incident as an excuse to invade China. Mitsuhirato then reports Tintin as a spy. Taking pity on Didi's mother, Tintin decides to find help for her son: Professor Fan Se-Yeng (Fang Hsi-Ying). Tintin sneaks into the International Settlement, but its corrupt Chief of Police, Dawson, hands him back to the Japanese. Tintin is condemned to death but is rescued by the Sons of the Dragon. Still on Fang Hsi-Ying's trail, Tintin travels to Hou-Kou. He rescues a young orphaned Chinese boy, Tchang. Tintin and Tchang eventually return to Shanghai after evading the Thompsons. Hiding at the Blue Lotus, Tintin overhears Mitsuhirato's plans but it is a trap and he is captured. Mitsuhirato reveals the secret leader of the Kih-Oskh conspiracy: Rastapopoulos. Tchang and his friends rescue Tintin and capture the villains. When Japan's machinations are exposed, Mitsuhirato commits hara-kiri. Professor Fang Hsi-Ying cures Didi and Tchang is adopted by Wang Chen-Yee.

Characters: As a brilliant testimonial to his friend's

influence, Hergé made Tchang one of the heroes of *The Blue Lotus*. The young Chinese orphan's relevance to the plot is slim, even though he helps save Tintin several times, but his endearing personality shines through to such an extent that no reader has ever questioned Tintin's almost obsessive devotion to his friend in *Tintin In Tibet*.

Dawson, the Chief of Police of the Shanghai International Settlement, and American businessman Gibbons of the American & Chinese Steel Company (offices in New York and Shanghai), are perhaps the two most despicable characters in the book. Rastapopoulos is a criminal mastermind, and Mitsuhirato at least has the excuse of patriotism for his crimes. But Dawson is simply corrupt and Gibbons is a loathsome bigot. This sharply contrasts with the nobility of the Chinese characters, such as the wise Wang Chen-Yee.

Continuity: The Blue Lotus concludes the 'Tintin In the Orient' arc and reveals the identity of the mysterious mastermind who had plagued Tintin since Port-Saïd: Rastapopoulos. He, Captain Allan and Dawson eventually returned in *The Red Sea Sharks*. Tchang's importance in Tintin's (and Hergé's) life became the subject of *Tintin In Tibet*. The Thompsons make a return appearance and apologise to Tintin – they never thought him guilty, but had to obey their orders.

Influences: 'Torn From Today's Headlines' is how one would describe *The Blue Lotus* now. There is no doubt that Hergé took China seriously and, with Tchang's help, presented not only a documented look at its

people and culture but also grappled with the hot political issues of the day. The pulpish elements of the earlier
stories are still there, but they are now relegated to mere
background – even a set-up as exotic as the Blue Lotus
is barely exploited and serves as a mere convenience.

Trivia: The Blue Lotus' openly pro-Chinese stance
caused the Japanese Consul in Brussels to issue a protest
after the story appeared in *Le Petit Vingtième*. The railroad sabotage blamed on Chinese bandits was, in fact,
based on the real incident at Moukden on 18
September 1931, which was used by Japan to justify its
invasion of China. Later, Hergé received an invitation
from Mrs Tchang Kai-Chek to visit China.

Only one material change was made between the
original black & white and the 1946 redrawn, coloured
versions of *The Blue Lotus*: removing the brief appearance of a gangster who showed up at the last minute
after Tintin and Tchang had already captured the main
villains.

Review: The Blue Lotus is unarguably Hergé's first
masterpiece. Tchang Tchong-Jen's influence was deep
and lasting. The book reflects a sudden awareness of the
reality and value of other cultures. Gibbons' bigoted
speech about bringing the benefits of western civilisation to China is almost word for word the type of
speech found in *Tintin In the Congo*, except that this
time, the roles are reversed, and Hergé's point of view
is deeply critical. Hergé goes on to mock the Chinese
clichés – Fu-Manchu moustaches and the like – again
a 180–degree turnabout from his earlier books.

Hergé's self-awareness extends to his own work: the

need to be accurate and truthful overrides the desire to spin a good yarn. *The Blue Lotus* attempts to portray China as it is, not as Belgians see it. Graphically, this meant obtaining accurate documentation instead of relying on colourful pre-digested press articles. In terms of story, it meant relying on real news instead of movie serials. For the first time, one senses that the story has become important. The book is still comprised of a series of not-too-tightly connected sequences, but there is an overall arc. And more importantly, there is a point. Tintin no longer wanders in and out of peril, he has a purpose, a mission.

As he had done in *Tintin In America* in the scene where the Indians were expropriated, Hergé uses a similar compression of time to show how Mitsuhirato's sabotage, inflated by the Japanese propaganda machine, becomes an act of war, reported all over the world, and justifying a subsequent invasion, all in half a page!

Because of the nature of its subject, *The Blue Lotus* improves when read in its original black & white version. Hergé has distilled his line to the essentials, and it is with this book that his brush acquires that wonderful precision that characterises his style. Many single panels have a beautiful, illustrative quality, purposefully evocative of Chinese art, while at the same time contributing to the overall dynamics of the story-telling. 4/5.

overhears it. Days later, Alonzo and Ramon are aboard a ship en route to San Theodoros. They kill Baltazar's murderer, but are exposed by Tintin. However, the arresting officer turns out to be their crony. Tintin is made to disembark, arrested and is about to be shot when a series of coups erupt, ending up with him being mistaken for a hero by General Alcazar. Alcazar makes Tintin a colonel. Later, Mr Chicklet from General American Oil tries to bribe Tintin to start a war with the neighbouring state of Nuevo Rico in order to control the Gran Chapo province and its oil reserves. Tintin refuses. With the help of gun merchant Basil Bazaroff, Chicklet frames Tintin for spying. Tintin escapes and, seeking to learn the fetish's secret, goes into the jungle where he meets an explorer, Ridgewell, who lives among the Arumbayas. Tintin learns that the man who took the fetish stole a sacred diamond which he hid inside the idol. Tintin returns to civilisation, after one more nasty encounter with Alonzo and Ramon. Back in Europe, Tintin discovers that the real fetish was found by Baltazar's brother and sold to an American millionaire. Tintin catches up with Alonzo and Ramon just as they steal the fetish. During the fight, the fetish is broken, Tintin, the two villains and the diamond fall into the sea; Tintin is rescued but the others drown. The millionaire asks him to take the repaired fetish back to the museum.

Characters: The Broken Ear introduced General Alcazar, a volatile, venal and dangerous man, who is certainly not a hero, but cannot entirely be considered as an outright villain either. Alcazar's obsession is to rule

San Theodoros. His perennial rival, General Tapioca, is mentioned but was not shown until *Tintin and the Picaros*. Also, what is it with Hergé and parrots? Another annoying parrot features prominently in the first third of the book.

Continuity: The Thompsons make a brief, perfunctory appearance at the beginning of the book. General Alcazar went on to make several return appearances, next to be seen in *The Seven Crystal Balls*.

Influences: The notion of a jewel hidden inside an idol which various parties try to possess at all costs is hardly an original idea. One is tempted to wonder whether Hergé had heard of Dashiell Hammett's 1929 novel *The Maltese Falcon*, which had already been filmed as *The Maltese Falcon* (aka *Dangerous Female*) in 1931 starring Ricardo Cortez and Bebe Daniels?

In any event, as was the case with Hitchcock's notorious 'MacGuffins', what is important here is not what moves the plot but what surrounds it. *The Broken Ear*, like *The Blue Lotus*, is a thinly-disguised mirror image of the political realities of the region. In this book, Hergé focuses his attention on the chaos and turmoil of South American politics and, in particular, on the real-life, three-year war which opposed Bolivia to Paraguay from 1932 to 1935 over the region of El Gran Chaco. As in the book, that war was also the result of political manipulations by western oil companies, and killed over 100,000 men.

Trivia: The character of international gun merchant Bazil Bazaroff is a transparent version of the real-life Basil Zaharoff (1850–1936), born Basileios Zacharias in

Turkey, educated in England and best remembered in connection with the Vickers-Armstrong munitions firm – renamed Vicking Arms in the book.

The Arumbaya fetish was copied by Hergé from an original pre-Columbian Peruvian idol. The original, as well as several copies, were exhibited in Brussels in 1979 as part of a *Tintin* retrospective. In a strange, life-imitating-fiction stunt, the main copy was mysteriously stolen and has never been recovered.

Finally, Hergé had drawn a frightening scene in the opening pages of the original black & white edition, showing Tintin having a nightmare in which an Arumbaya Indian stepped into his bedroom and shot him with a poison arrow – strangely similar to scenes from *Cigars of the Pharaoh* and *The Seven Crystal Balls*. It was, however, removed from the 1943 redrawn version.

Review: Tintin and the Broken Ear is a little like a *Blue Lotus*-lite. The adventure, the dastardly villains, the political drama, the wild pursuits, all the traditional ingredients are present, but it is not cast in as dramatic and emotional a light. The tragedy of banana republics going to war for the sake of ruthless oil interests is exposed. Hergé uses the same ellipse device to show Bazaroff selling the arms to both rival countries. But the colourful antics of the natives with their five-minute revolutions and comical bombs mitigate the seriousness of the situation and are more reminiscent of the earlier, more caricatured books.

The Broken Ear, however, shows a marked improvement in Hergé's plotting skills. Gone are the loosely connected series of incidents without a unifying thread. This time, Hergé uses a single device – the fetish – to propel his plot and stays with it until the end. It makes for a very effective, dramatic story, with plenty of twists and betrayals, centring around an obsessive and ultimately deadly and just as pointless pursuit of wealth.

Graphically, *The Broken Ear* is in the straight continuity of *The Blue Lotus*, and does not innovate in any particular respect. However, one has to give credit to Hergé for having created a modern visual icon with his unforgettable image of the fetish with the broken ear. 2/5.

The Black Island

Publishing History:

1. Serialisation in Belgium in *Le Petit Vingtième* from 15 April 1937, and in France in *Coeurs Vaillants* under the title *Le Mystère de L'Avion Gris* (*The Mystery of the Grey Plane*) from 17 April 1938.
2. *L'Île Noire*, 124 pages, black & white, Editions Casterman, Tournai, 1938.
3. *L'Île Noire*, 62 pages, colour, Editions Casterman, Tournai, 1943.
4. *L'Île Noire*, modernised redrawn version (with Bob De Moor), serialisation in *Tintin* from May, 1965 (Nos. 663–893).
5. *L'Île Noire*, modernised redrawn version (with Bob De Moor), 62 pages, colour, Editions Casterman, Tournai, 1966.

6. In *Archives Hergé*, Volume 4, Editions Casterman, Tournai, 1980.
7. *L'Île Noire*, facsimile edition of 2, Editions Casterman, Tournai, 1987.

The Black Island ran in *Le Petit Vingtième* from 15 April 1937 to 16 November 1938. The first hardcover collection was published by Casterman in 1938. It was then reformatted and coloured by Hergé in 1943.

However, in the mid-1960s, when the time came to prepare an English translation for the United Kingdom, Hergé's translators, Leslie Lonsdale-Cooper and Michael Turner, pointed out both the errors and the dated characteristics of the book. Hergé decided to update the story and dispatched his assistant, Bob De Moor, on a research trip to England and Scotland. De Moor returned with enough new material to prepare an entirely redrawn and modernised third version of the story, which was released in 1966.

The original black & white edition was eventually reprinted in the fourth volume of *Archives Hergé* in 1980. A true facsimile of the original edition was published in 1987.

Plot: Tintin is shot while trying to help two mysterious aviators. When the Thompsons tell him that the same plane later crashed in Sussex, he travels to England to investigate but the villains' ringleader, Wronzoff (Puschov), is worried that he is onto them. First, they try to frame him, then to kill him on the cliffs of Dover. Thanks to Snowy, Tintin escapes and eventually the trail leads him to the house of Dr Muller. A fire starts during Tintin's ensuing fight with Muller and his driver, Ivan, but Tintin is rescued by the local firemen. Later, he discovers that a plane is dropping bags of forged banknotes on the property at night. Tintin pursues Muller and Ivan by plane to Scotland but loses them in the fog. He travels to Kiltoch, where he learns of the 'Black Island' and of its castle, supposedly haunted by a mysterious 'Beast.' Tintin goes to the Black Island where he confronts Puschov and the 'Beast' – a tame gorilla named Ranko, who turns out to be afraid of Snowy! – and discovers the forgers' secret HQ. Tintin single-handedly outwits the forgers and radios Scotland Yard for help. The gang is arrested and Tintin makes the headlines.

Characters: The Black Island introduced yet another recurring villain, Dr Muller, who returned in *Land of Black Gold* and *The Red Sea Sharks* as Mull-Pacha, and was inspired by the real-life British officer, Sir John Bagot Glubb (1897–1986) also known as Glubb Pacha.

Continuity: The Thompsons again try to arrest Tintin for a crime he did not commit but this time their hearts really are not in it. Since Dr Muller is taken to jail at the end of the story and justice is not kind to counterfeiters, one wonders how he found himself at large in the Middle East only two years later in 1939 in the first version of *Land of Black Gold* – unless he staged a daring escape, of course. When Bob De Moor redrew *The Black Island*, he retroactively replaced the original journalists interviewing the old man on page 61 with the two journalists from *Paris-Flash* introduced in *The Castafiore Emerald*.

Influences: Villains using superstition to hide their lair was, as pointed out earlier, something that popped up regularly in serials and comic strips, whether in the form of gangsters wearing bed sheets to pose as ghosts, or cardboard monsters scaring onlookers away. Hergé had used the concept in *Tintin In the Land of the Soviets.* Jean Ray used a fake Loch Ness-like monster to hide a German submarine in a Scottish loch in one of his *Harry Dickson* pulp adventures, *La Pieuvre Noire* (*The Black Octopus,* No. 95, 1933). Here, it is a trained gorilla that plays the part of the creature. Perhaps a reminiscence of the popular *King Kong* (1933)? Or more likely of Gaston Leroux' murderous gorilla *Balaoo* (1911), filmed in 1913.

Trivia: Hergé showed some forward-thinking in showing Tintin watching the Thompsons air acrobatics on a television at the end of the book. By 1937, television was still a relatively new phenomenon, and the BBC was only broadcasting a dozen hours or so a week. Amusingly, the television image is shown in colour in the 1943 version, but in black & white in the 1966 version! The counterfeit notes were also upgraded from one pound to five pounds.

Review: *The Black Island* is a clever little thriller presented against a mild fantasy background, which is of course explained away at the end. It is the type of story that was popular in the detective serials of the times, from Edgar Wallace to Leslie Charteris, but was not generally seen in the tamer, children-oriented comics. The hard-boiled edge in *The Black Island* is more evident than in *The Broken Ear.* In the story, the villains, and more surprisingly Tintin, do not hesitate to use their guns to threaten to kill their enemies. Of course, Tintin does not kill but to see him point a gun at two men while saying, 'one more step and you're dead' (page 50) is a bit of a shock. This was, in fact, softened to "get back and put up your hands!" in the English edition.

The Black Island is part of the pre-war *Petit Vingtième*, which goes from *The Broken Ear* to *King Ottokar's Sceptre*. Hergé was comfortable with his style and his format and had not yet been forced to adjust to the demands of other formats. The original version of the book, and its first redrawn and coloured edition, are therefore very much in the same continuity as its predecessor and successor. The 1966 redrawn version, however, is almost an entirely different book. The story gained in slickness – the backgrounds are superb and the images of Tintin arriving in Kiltoch or disembarking on the Black Island are beautiful – but it lost some of its atmosphere. 2/5.

King Ottokar's Sceptre

Publishing History:

1. Serialisation in Belgium in *Le Petit Vingtième* under the title *Tintin en Syldavie* (*Tintin In Syldavia*) from 4 August 1938, and in France in *Coeurs Vaillants* from 14 May 1939.
2. *Le Sceptre D'Ottokar*, 120 pages, black & white, Editions Casterman, Tournai, 1939.
3. *Le Sceptre D'Ottokar*, 62 pages, colour, Editions Casterman, Tournai, 1947.

4. In *Archives Hergé*, Volume 4, Editions Casterman, Tournai, 1980.
5. *Le Sceptre D'Ottokar*, facsimile edition of 2, Editions Casterman, Tournai, 1988.

King Ottokar's Sceptre was the last of the *Tintin* stories to be published in *Le Petit Vingtième*, from 4 August 1938 to 10 August 1939. Casterman published the original black & white edition in 1939, then a colour edition considerably redrawn by Edgar P Jacobs in 1947. The original black & white edition was eventually reprinted in the fourth volume of *Archives Hergé* in 1980. A true facsimile of the original edition was published in 1988.

Plot: Tintin becomes friend with Professor Halembique (Alembick), who is about to travel to Syldavia (a middle-European country locked in a struggle with its neighbour, Borduria) to study ancient seals. Alembick is under surveillance by Syldavian spies who repeatedly try to get rid of Tintin. Tintin leaves with Alembick for Syldavia. The pilot of the plane jettisons Tintin but he lands safely in a haystack. He makes his way to the capital, Klow, meeting the notorious opera singer Bianca Castafiore; but the villains, who have infiltrated even the Syldavian police, try to stop him at every turn. Tintin attempts to see King Muskar but is foiled by his aide-de-camp, Colonel Boris Jorgen, also a traitor. In the end, Tintin succeeds in gaining the King's confidence, but is too late to stop Alembick from mysteriously stealing the Sceptre. Without it, the King will be deposed and Borduria will invade. Tintin discovers how the Sceptre was stolen and, with the

Thompsons' help, follows the thieves back to the Bordurian border. He succeeds in reclaiming the Sceptre and manages to make it back to Klow to save the kingdom in the nick of time. The traitors are arrested, Borduria pulls back its troops and Tintin is awarded a medal. The police explain that Alembick was replaced by his evil twin brother just before they all left for Syldavia.

Characters: The major character introduced in *King Ottokar's Sceptre*, albeit very briefly, is the formidable opera singer Bianca Castafiore, the 'Milanese Nightingale,' and her then unnamed accompanying pianist, Igor Wagner. The 'jewel' song from Gounod's *Faust* is the ultimate weapon in her repertoire and hearing it in close quarters is enough to make Tintin choose risking death at the hands of his enemies by leaving her car.

A dastardly villain making his first appearance in *King Ottokar's Sceptre* is the traitorous Colonel Boris Jorgen, but in reality, the real villains are the Bordurians and the unseen Musstler, a transparent combination of Mussolini and Hitler, the leader of the SS-like Iron Guard, who are plotting the takeover of Syldavia.

Continuity: King Ottokar's Sceptre introduces the countries of Syldavia and Borduria, which later took centre stage in *Destination Moon* and *The Calculus Affair.* Hergé provided so much background information on Syldavian culture and language that fans have since compiled Syldavian grammars and dictionaries, as is the case with Tolkien's Elvish and Star Trek's Klingon languages.

The Castafiore continued to plague Tintin and, especially, Captain Haddock in later books. The traitorous Colonel Jorgen returned in *Explorers on the Moon*.

Influences: Anthony Hope's *The Prisoner of Zenda* (1894) had been filmed in 1913, 1915, 1922 and 1937 – the superb John Cromwell version with Ronald Coleman – and had popularised Ruritania-type kingdoms in pulp literature. To name but a few, Arsène Lupin had visited the fictional Duchy of Veldenz in *813* (1910), Fantômas had kidnapped the king of the equally fictional Hesse-Weimar in *Un Roi Prisonnier de Fantômas* (*A King Prisoner of Fantômas*, 1911) and even Mickey Mouse had impersonated the King of Medioka in *Mickey His Royal Highness* in 1937!

What makes Syldavia (originally named Sylduria) different from any of the above is its connection to the very real and frightening possibility of a forced annexation by its neighbour, Borduria, a Nazi-like country in all but name. The Annexation of Austria by Hitler's Germany had taken place on 11 and 12 March 1938, only a few months before *King Ottokar's Sceptre* began its run. Hergé's forceful warning against Musstler, his tactics and his goals, however, went unnoticed. They certainly were not credited to his political account by those who later accused him of collaboration after World War Two.

Trivia: Edgar P Jacobs redesigned much of the original black & white edition for the colour edition of 1947, in particular the costumes of the Syldavian guards, who had originally looked like British Beefeaters, were given a balkanised look. Jacobs drew himself and his wife among the dignitaries attending Tintin's triumph at the end (on page 59). He is the breast-plated nobleman accompanied by a lady in a blue dress on the right.

Review: King Ottokar's Sceptre is a Hitchcockian thriller in which Tintin is virtually alone, trying to save an opera kingdom from the jaws of the Nazi beast. Even the kind Professor Alembick becomes the target of his suspicion when, *Invaders*-like, Tintin knows that he is no longer the same man, but cannot prove it. There is a traitor at every corner and the tightly-controlled plot recaptures the paranoid ambience that Hergé had used to good effect in *Cigars of the Pharaoh*.

Then, the book turns into a fascinating 'locked room' mystery: how could the Sceptre have been spirited away? The resolution is ingeniously clever. Finally, the third act is an *Indiana Jones*-like race against the clock: if Tintin does not get the sceptre back to the King in time, the Kingdom is doomed. Like Spielberg, Hergé uses every trick to pull the reader's heartstrings. In the end, it is brave, devoted Snowy who arrives at the very last minute with the Sceptre, saving the day!

At the same time, one admires Hergé's legerdemain in keeping the real stakes in this game visually offstage. Unlike *The Blue Lotus*, we don't see much of the Bordurians – a border post and a one-panel admission of defeat at the end. Musstler is kept carefully under wraps. The horrors of the real world may lurk in the background but they are not allowed to interfere with the pure escapist nature of the adventure.

The black & white edition is quite serviceable for

the period, but Jacobs' excellent redesign of the Syldavians makes the original colour edition better. The three pages of a tourist brochure providing information on Syldavia are a gem. The Sceptre itself may not have the sheer iconic appeal of the fetish with the broken ear but, as a MacGuffin, it serves its purpose well. 3/5.

The Crab with the Golden Claws

Publishing History:
1. Serialisation in Belgium in *Le Soir Jeunesse* then *Le Soir* from 17 October 1940, and in France in *Coeurs Vaillants* from 21 June 1942.
2. *Le Crabe aux Pinces D'Or*, 120 pages, black & white, Editions Casterman, Tournai, 1941.
3. *Le Crabe aux Pinces D'Or*, 62 pages, colour, Editions Casterman, Tournai, 1944.
4. In *Archives Hergé*, Volume 4, Editions Casterman, Tournai, 1980.
5. *Le Crabe aux Pinces D'Or*, facsimile edition of 2, Editions Casterman, Tournai, 1989.

After *King Ottokar's Sceptre*, Hergé began his next saga, *The Land of Black Gold*, which ran for 58 pages in *Le Petit Vingtième* from 28 September 1939 to 8 May 1940. In the meantime, Hergé had been mobilised in the Belgian army, but continued to send his two-page weekly instalments. On 9 May 1940, as a result of the Nazi invasion of Belgium, *Le Vingtième Siècle* and its weekly children's supplement were discontinued and *Land of Black Gold* was left uncompleted.

Hergé, who had been let out of the army for health reasons in April 1940, stayed briefly in France then returned to Belgium, where he began working for the daily newspaper *Le Soir* (*Evening Times*). Because of Tintin's fame, *Le Soir* decided to launch a children's supplement, *Le Soir Jeunesse*, featuring *Tintin*. On 17 October 1940, *Tintin* made his return in an all-new story, *The Crab with the Golden Claws*.

Eventually, the same paper shortages that made Casterman ask Hergé to reformat his books to a lower page count of 62 pages, forced the cancellation of *Le Soir Jeunesse* on 3 September 1941. *The Crab with the Golden Claws* then moved to *Le Soir* on 23 September 1941, but in the form of daily strips.

Casterman eventually published a collection in the original black & white format, minus some strips, in 1941 then a colour edition in 1944. The original black & white edition was eventually reprinted in the fourth volume of *Archives Hergé* in 1980. A true facsimile of the original edition was published in 1989.

Plot: Tintin and the Thompsons investigate fake coins, which inadvertently puts Tintin on the trail of a tin can of crab with a torn label, on the back of which is written the word 'Karaboudjan.' This turns out to be the name of a ship. Tintin is taken prisoner aboard the ship, which is ruled by her lieutenant, Allan. The intrepid reporter discovers that the Karaboudjan is smuggling opium inside the cans of crab. Tintin only escapes thanks to the help of the well-meaning but hopelessly drunken Captain Haddock. After capturing the seaplane the villains sent after them, Tintin and

Haddock crash in the Sahara desert. They almost die of thirst but are rescued by the Foreign Legion. Later, after a battle with rebel tribes, they reach the city of Bagghar on the Moroccan coast. There, Tintin recognises Allan, even though the Karaboudjan is supposed to have been lost at sea. He again joins forces with the Thompsons. The villains kidnap Haddock after he recognises the Karaboudjan under another name. The trail leads Tintin and the Thompsons to the ringleader, a rich merchant named Omar Ben Salaad. Tintin enters the villains' underground lair and frees Haddock. Ben Salaad is arrested. Tintin chases and captures Allan after a speedy motor boat race.

Characters: Enter: Captain Haddock! More than a Tintin adventure, *The Crab with the Golden Claws* is the story of Haddock's redemption. When we first meet him, he is a pathetic figure, Allan's drunken puppet. When, thanks to Tintin, he discovers what he is, Haddock tries to regain control of his life but several times the need to drink turns this frail, sympathetic companion into a dangerous, drunken brute. Under the influence of alcohol, he sets fire to their lifeboat and causes the seaplane to crash. It is only after literally crossing the desert that Haddock redeems himself. His redemption comes on page 37 when he single-handedly confronts the rebel Berbers. The situation is both funny – what triggers him is a stray bullet breaking his last bottle – and moving. From a weak, unreliable man, he becomes a trusty ally on his way to recovery.

By contrast, Allan is a wily brute, who keeps beating up people, his own men included. He is the true villain of the book, far more than the rarely seen Omar Ben Salaad (his name means 'Lobster Salad'), a second-hand Rastapopoulos. Allan is starkly drawn by Hergé, who imbues him with a vicious energy that makes him a powerful threat. He exhibits, in turn, black-hearted rage and caustic humour. In *The Crab with the Golden Claws*, he emerges as a well-rounded, fully fleshed-out character.

Continuity: Allan was last seen employed by Rastapopoulos in *Cigars of the Pharaoh*. Neither Tintin nor he appear to recognise each other but their initial encounter was so brief and under such circumstances – Tintin was prisoner in a sarcophagus that Allan dumped at sea – that such ignorance is believable. Allan returned in *The Red Sea Sharks*, again as Rastapopoulos's henchman, but was not as terrifying as he is here.

Influences: Christopher Wren's novel *Beau Geste* (1925) virtually created the myth of the French Foreign Legion, popularised in three movie adaptations, in 1916, 1928 (as *Beau Sabreur*) and 1939, the last two with Gary Cooper. Even Mickey joined the Foreign Legion in *Mickey In the Foreign Legion* in 1936.

Otherwise, *The Crab with the Golden Claws* is a thinly-disguised remake of *Cigars of the Pharaoh*. In the former, opium is smuggled in cigars, in the latter, in tins of crab. Both cigars and tins bear a cryptic logo: the Sign of Kih-Oskh, tattooed on Rastapopoulos's arm, in the former, and the Golden Claws, hanging on Ben Salaad's neck, in the latter. Both stories involve desert treks, hostile tribes and, at the end, the infiltrating of a secret underground lair. *Cigars* ends on a high-speed car race in the mountains, *Crab* on a high-speed boat race at sea.

Trivia: Anti-alcoholic forces objected to panels of Captain Haddock actually drinking from the bottle on page 19, so these were changed. More curiously, it has been reported that a black henchman of Allan on page 53 was changed to a Moroccan because some parties in America were concerned that white men (even villains) should not be shown associating with blacks!

Review: The Nazi invasion of Belgium caused the cancellation of *Le Vingtième Siècle* and the banning of two of Hergé's books, *Tintin In America* and *The Black Island*, because of their respective connections to America and England. Surprisingly, no one appears to have noticed the virulent anti-fascism of *King Ottokar's Sceptre*!

Seeking to avoid suspect themes, Hergé carefully moved his story to the exotic Sahara locale, although even there, his highly sympathetic portrayal of the French Foreign Legion could have been seen as questionable by the Occupiers. One is puzzled by the revelation at the end of the book, of a mysterious Asian character, first shown being kidnapped by the villains in the first pages. He is shown to be a detective from Yokohama, Japan, on the trail of the opium smugglers. That revelation makes no sense, whether in light of the events of *The Blue Lotus*, in which the Japanese were depicted as being behind opium smuggling, or even in the context of the times.

Artistically, *The Crab with the Golden Claws* is a turning point in Hergé's career. From a regular two-page weekly schedule, he was made to switch to a daily strip, which forced him to change his storytelling technique. As a result, the last third of the book seems rushed, compared to the more leisurely pace of the beginning. Another consequence of that change was that when the 1944 Casterman edition had to be compiled, Hergé was short of pages. So he used four full-page illustrations, of the type previously left unused in the earlier books, to make up pages 21, 29, 40 and 49. Graphically, the most interesting note is the presence of another short but remarkably surreal dream sequence on page 32. It, too, features Haddock. Ultimately, his appearance is the most memorable aspect of this transitional work. 3/5.

The Shooting Star

Publishing History:
1. Serialisation in Belgium in *Le Soir* from 20 October 1941, and in France in *Coeurs Vaillants* from 6 June 1943.
2. *L'Étoile Mystérieuse*, 62 pages, colour, Editions Casterman, Tournai, 1942.

L'Étoile Mystérieuse ran in *Le Soir* from 20 October 1941 to 21 May 1942 and was the first *Tintin* book to be published by Casterman directly in colour in the 62-page format.

Plot: An asteroid is about to crash into the Earth and everyone is afraid that the end of the world is near. The asteroid misses the Earth but a piece of it, an aerolith, falls into the Northern Atlantic, near the Arctic Circle. Astronomer Hyppolyte Calys (Decimus Phostle) discovers the presence of a new element, which he christens 'calystene,' on the fragment. A scientific expedition is launched aboard the ship Aurora, captained by Haddock, to claim the aerolith. But a competing expedition, financed by the banker Bohlwinkel, uses sabotage and dirty tricks to stop the Aurora and ensure that its own ship, the Peary, is the first to reach the aerolith. Tintin, however, parachutes on the island-size aerolith, and claims it first by unfurling his expedition flag just before the competition arrives. The aerolith is the site of mysterious calystene-induced phenomena: giant, exploding mushrooms, things growing at a rapid pace and reaching gigantic proportions, including a monstrous spider. Eventually, the aerolith sinks beneath the sea; Tintin and Snowy are rescued just in the nick of time and bring back a calystene rock for further study.

Characters: Captain Haddock makes a responsible return. While still weak when it comes to the occasional drink, he is no longer the pathetic wreck first seen in *The Crab with the Golden Claws*. This is the definitive version of Haddock that we have come to know and love. After Prof. Sarcophagus of *Cigars of the Pharaoh*, Professor Phostle is another interesting attempt by Hergé to create an eccentric scientist in the Jules Verne tradition. Phostle is just as crazy and self-centred as Tournesol (Calculus), but more one-dimensional. Interestingly enough, he was scheduled to return in an earlier version of *Destination Moon* that Hergé and Van

Melkebeke planned at the time. In addition to Tintin, Haddock and Phostle, the other members of the Aurora expedition are from Germany, Portugal, Spain, Sweden and Switzerland.

Mad, apocalyptic prophet Philippulus is an unforgettable character, displaying the same surreal sense of insanity that surrounded Sarcophagus in *Cigars of the Pharaoh*.

Continuity: We meet one of Haddock's old friends, Captain Chester, mentioned in later books. Swiss team member Prof. Cantonneau returned in *The Seven Crystal Balls*.

Influences: Hergé always denied having read more than one of Jules Verne's novels, and that with only little attention. Yet, the fact remains that, not only the plot, but many of the details of *The Shooting Star* are similar to Verne's *La Chasse au Météore* (*The Chase of the Golden Meteor*, 1908), in which rival expeditions try to seize control of a meteor fragment that sank in the North Atlantic. Verne's eccentric scientist is Zephyrin Xirdal, Hergé's Hyppolyte Calys; Verne's new element, xirdalium, Hergé's calystene; Verne's villain is banker JBK Lowenthal, Hergé's Blumenstein (in the original version). Incredibly, both books have in their respective expeditions a Doktor (Professor in *The Shooting Star*) Schultze (Schulze in *The Shooting Star*) of the University of Iena in Germany! Some scholars have attributed such similarities in the *Tintin* story to the influence of Hergé's friend, writer–journalist Jacques Van Melkebeke. Van Melkebeke and Hergé wrote two *Tintin* plays together that same year. Van Melkebeke was said to be both instrumental in helping Hergé plot his stories and far better acquainted with fantasy literature.

Trivia: When the book was first put together in 1942, Hergé removed a panel that had appeared in the daily strip in *Le Soir* that showed two very caricatured Jews speculating on the end of the world.

In 1954, *The Shooting Star* underwent a number of cosmetic changes to make the story more 'politically correct,' as we would put it today. The villainous banker Blumenstein was renamed Bohlwinkel (after the word 'bolewinkel' meaning a candy store). The villains' country was changed from the United States to the fictional Sao Rico and the villains' flag from the Stars & Stripes to an imaginary flag – even though, due to an omission, the American flag can still be seen flying over the Peary on page 35, panel 8.

Quick & Flupke and the Thompsons appear on page 20.

Review: First, let us dispense with the surface of the book: the fantasy elements are brought in convincingly and make for a welcome change in what had been, until now, a series of crime thrillers. The pre-apocalyptic ambience is stark and believable. Once again, Hergé's keen visual instincts enabled him to craft some truly unforgettable images, such as the wonderful, red and white exploding mushrooms of the aerolith – a strange anticipation of the nuclear mushroom-shaped cloud – and the giant spider which threatens Tintin.

Still, *The Shooting Star* remains to this day a blot on Hergé's record. How did the man who had so eloquently defended the Native Americans in *Tintin In*

America and the Chinese in *The Blue Lotus*, who only three years before denounced fascism in *King Ottokar's Sceptre*, become a propagandist for the Axis remains hard to understand. It did not have to be that way. Unlike *The Shooting Star*, the next two *Tintin* stories, also written and drawn during the time of Belgian occupation, did not concern themselves with politics. *The Shooting Star*, sadly, did.

Tintin's expedition is clearly an Axis-sponsored mission – its members are all from Axis or neutral countries, and even its seaplane is a German Arado 193. Its ruthless opponents are the United States and International Jewry. They are shown ready to use any means, including sinking the Aurora and its passengers, to achieve their ends. The anti-Semitic charge must also take into consideration the offensive panel from the daily strip removed from the book, for which there is no justification, story-wise or of any other kind.

From Shakespeare's Shylock to Jules Verne's Isac Hakhabut in *Hector Servadac* (1877), the figure of the odious Jew was, sadly, well entrenched in fiction, even in the works of authors who clearly were not anti-Semitic. To some extent, one should take into account the context of the times and the ignorance of the Holocaust before rushing to judgement. But even if Hergé was not anti-Semitic, he was toeing the Nazi Party's line, which is hardly better, and in the context of a children's strip, rather surprising.

Hergé later defended his Blumenstein as being a caricature, just as, say, his Mitsuhirato was a caricature of the Japanese, and his Alcazar a caricature of the South

Americans. That 'equal opportunity' argument has merit. But then, does this mean that *The Shooting Star* portrays Jews and America in the same fashion as, say, *The Blue Lotus* portrays Mitsuhirato and Japan? If so, that analogy is historically wrong, especially in the context of the times. The evils of multinational corporations are not to be balanced against the evils of fascism.

Hergé had attacked American capitalism before: in *Cigars*, Rastapopoulos is obviously an American; in *The Blue Lotus* and *The Broken Ear*, the villainous Gibbons and Chicklet embody the rapacity and lack of scruples of American businesses abroad. Even Chicklet's British oil rival is not too different from Blumenstein, whose bank controls the Golden Oil Company...

Such political positions were characteristic of French and Belgian pro-clerical, right-wing movements, similarly opposed to socialism from the east and capitalism from the west. There were, and still are today, many advocates for these ideas and sometimes the line between anti-Americanism, anti-capitalism, anti-socialism and anti-Semitism becomes blurred. At the extremes, one finds the Nazi ideology and their ilk. The issue here, however, is not to debate the merits of Hergé's position on the subject but to acknowledge it for what it was.

What is, to some extent, more damning is the blissful ignorance, or state of denial, exhibited by Hergé long after these issues were far less debatable. First, he waited until 1954 to remove the offensive material from the book. Ironically, the change from Blumenstein to

Bohlwinkel did not make matters better as the latter patronym is also Jewish. Second, when confronted with the issue in Benoît Peeters' *Le Monde D'Hergé* (page 111), Hergé equalled the Blumenstein/Bohlwinkel 'unfortunate' incident (to say the least!) with the fact that his design of the Aurora was inaccurate, and that a ship like that could not have sailed. To state that this shows an appalling lack of understanding is an understatement.

In the end, we are left with the fact that the man who was willing to have the entire *Black Island* book redrawn because of some trivial objections by his British translators, saw nothing wrong in leaving *The Shooting Star* stand more or less as it was. Yet, if ever a book begged to be redone, it was this one. To this day, *The Shooting Star* is sadly still used by extreme right-wing Nazi apologists and revisionists, such as the notorious French holocaust denier Olivier Mathieu, to bolster their ridiculous claim that Hergé was pro-Nazi and anti-Semite. Looking at his entire life, oeuvre and statements, he was not, but the existence of *The Shooting Star*, and Hergé's subsequent inability to deal with it, are sad moments in *Tintin*'s history. 1/5.

The Secret of the Unicorn
Red Rackham's Treasure

Publishing History:
1. *Le Secret de la Licorne*, serialisation in Belgium in *Le Soir* from 11 June 1942, and in France in *Coeurs Vaillants* from 19 March 1944.

2. *Le Trésor de Rackham le Rouge*, serialisation in Belgium in *Le Soir* from 19 February 1943.
3. *Le Secret de la Licorne*, 62 pages, colour, Editions Casterman, Tournai, 1943.
4. *Le Trésor de Rackham le Rouge*, 62 pages, colour, Editions Casterman, Tournai, 1944.

Secret of the Unicorn and *Red Rackham's Treasure* ran entirely in *Le Soir* in the form of daily strips, before being collected in colour by Casterman.

Plot: Tintin meets the Thompsons at a flea market; they are on the trail of an elusive pickpocket. Tintin buys a model of a seventeenth-century ship, the Licorne (Unicorn) as a gift for Captain Haddock. Two other parties seem desperate to buy it from him but he refuses. It turns out that Tintin's Unicorn is part of a set of three model ships. The Captain recognises the ship as the one captained by his seventeenth-century ancestor, and proceeds to tell Tintin about how the Unicorn was captured by the pirate Red Rackham. But the Captain's ancestor escaped with Red Rackham's treasure and blew up the ship. Tintin now believes that the secret of the treasure's location is contained on small scrolls hidden inside the models. Tintin's two buyers are attacked by the Loiseau (Bird) brothers, who kidnap Tintin and keep him prisoner inside their castle at Moulinsart (Marlinspike). Tintin escapes and eventually captures the brothers, but one escapes. Two of the missing scrolls are eventually found in a wallet stolen from one of the Bird brothers by the pickpocket. The other Bird is finally arrested and the first scroll recovered. When superimposed on each other the scrolls reveal the location of the island where the Unicorn was sunk – and where Red Rackham's treasure may wait.

The second book opens with the final preparations of an expedition led by Tintin and Haddock aboard the ship Sirius to find Red Rackham's treasure. An eccentric scientist, Tryphon Tournesol (Cuthbert Calculus), tries to interest them in a shark-shaped pocket submarine but they turn him down. The Thompsons join the expedition to protect it from one of the Bird Brothers who escaped from jail. They later discover that Calculus stowed away with his submarine. Eventually, they find the island where the Captain's ancestor sank the Unicorn and locate traces of his stay there. Later, they find the wreck of the sunken ship and recover pirate artefacts and a chest with ancient documents, but no treasure. They dejectedly return to Europe. As they explore Marlinspike, revealed by the documents to be Haddock's ancestral home, Tintin finally finds the treasure which had been hidden there all the time. Calculus buys Marlinspike for Haddock with the proceeds from the sale of his submarine.

Characters: The *Red Rackham* story arc introduces the Castle of Marlinspike, modelled after that of Cheverny on the Loire river. The original name, Moulinsart, is an anagram of the real village of Sarmoulin. With the castle comes faithful butler Nestor, who in the first book unwittingly serves the two villainous Bird Brothers, but who soon transfers his loyalty to Haddock after he buys the castle.

By far the best realised character in the first book is

Haddock's ancestor, the Chevalier François de Haddoque, a wonderfully colourful figure, a great sailor and swordsman, and a wily rascal. The Bird brothers are relatively uninspired villains in Tintin's Rogues Gallery. The kleptomaniac pickpocket, whose identity is revealed at the end as that of a meek and honourable-looking retired civil servant, is a far more colourful and interesting character.

The second book introduced Professor Calculus, after which *Tintin* was never the same. A combination of Professor Alembick of *King Ottokar's Sceptre* (with whom he shares the absent-mindedness) and Professor Phostle of *The Shooting Star* (for his scientific brilliance), Calculus was loosely inspired by the real-life Professor Picard, the inventor of the bathyscaphe, whose name also inspired Gene Roddenberry in the naming of the captain of *Star Trek: The Next Generation*. In the beginning, Calculus is no more than a mere hobbyist inventor, but his scientific knowledge and abilities increase by leaps and bounds in the series. Far from being a Mister Spock, however, he is a poet and a romantic. With Haddock, he completes the indispensable triangle that imbues *Tintin* with its mythic quality.

Continuity: The *Red Rackham* story arc is a turning point in the series because it shifts the focus away from Tintin. Captain Haddock is shown to be, by far, the more interesting character and the books give him roots, not only in the past but in the present with the introduction of Marlinspike. This time the Thompsons are an integral part of the story – they were absent from the earlier volume – and with the addition of Calculus, one senses that the Tintin family is at last complete.

The ship used by Tintin and his friends to go looking for the treasure is the Sirius, Captain Chester's ship in *The Shooting Star*.

Influences: A modern-day *Treasure Island* which starts with a clever puzzle, the *Red Rackham* story arc is pure adventure. Some scholars have noted the similarities between Tintin's three scrolls hidden in the Unicorns and the three scrolls found in a bottle in Jules Verne's *Les Enfants du Capitaine Grant* (*The Children of Captain Grant*, 1867), which also features a distracted scientist named Paganel.

Trivia: Hergé's friend, Jacques Van Melkebeke, is shown shopping at the flea market (the man in the brown suit in the foreground) in *The Secret of the Unicorn*, page 2, in the middle panel of the last strip.

Coincidentally, there were several authentic Captain Haddocks, the most distinguished being Sir Richard Haddock (1629–1715) of Leigh-on-Sea who captained the Royal James at the battle of Sole Bay.

Hergé pokes gentle fun at French comedian, writer and director Sacha Guitry by advertising a play simply entitled *Me* in which Mr Guitry plays all the roles on page 2 of *Red Rackham's Treasure*.

Calculus keeps saying throughout the book that the real location of the treasure is 'to the west' – yet, Marlinspike (where it is finally revealed to be) is to the East of the uncharted Island, clearly shown on the globe (page 61) to be in the Atlantic.

A strip removed from the book showed one of the Thompsons actually finding a silver button from the

Captain's ancestor's jacket buried near the cross on the island.

Finally, Tintin first adopted his familiar blue sweater and white shirt 'uniform' in *Red Rackham's Treasure*. Prior to this, his clothes were usually a yellow shirt and a brown suit.

Review: The *Red Rackham* story arc launches *Tintin's* best and greatest era. With the arrival of Prof. Calculus, the family of characters is now complete. The art has reached a degree of near-perfection; outside documentation is smoothly and unobtrusively integrated into the whole. The stories are not only tightly paced but their plots work like clockwork.

Hergé allegedly listed *The Secret of the Unicorn* as one of his favourite books – deservedly so because its storytelling is truly outstanding. The book intercuts three plot lines – the search for the scrolls, the mystery of the pickpocket and the retelling of the past – in an astounding display of style. The Captain's story is a superbly entertaining bit of swashbuckling and is cleverly counterpointed by the running gag of everything in it reminding Haddock of how thirsty he is.

In *Red Rackham's Treasure*, each character, Haddock, Calculus and the Thompsons, has his own story arc; yet, the focus on the main plot is never lost. The circularity of Tintin's quest for a treasure, a journey that takes him to the ends of the world only to return him to the point where he started, is pure magic. Again, we behold Hergé's astounding gift of creating unforgettable images: Tintin's undersea exploration aboard Prof. Calculus' shark-shaped submarine is yet another unique moment. *The Secret of the Unicorn*: 4/5; *Red Rackham's Treasure*: 5/5.

The Seven Crystal Balls
Prisoners of the Sun

Publishing History:

1. Serialisation in Belgium in *Le Soir* (as *Les Sept Boules de Cristal*) from 16 December 1943, interrupted on 2 September 1944, restarted in the Belgian edition of *Le Journal de Tintin* (as *Le Temple du Soleil*) from 26 September 1946; and in France in *Coeurs Vaillants* from 19 May 1946 (*Les Sept Boules de Cristal*) and 30 November 1947 (*Le Temple du Soleil*).

2. *Les Sept Boules de Cristal*, 62 pages, colour, Editions Casterman, Tournai, 1948.

3. *Le Temple du Soleil*, 62 pages, colour, Editions Casterman, Tournai, 1949.

Like its immediate predecessors, *The Seven Crystal Balls* first ran as a series of black & white daily strips in *Le Soir* from 16 December 1943 to 2 September 1944, at which time the liberation of Belgium by the Allies resulted in the firing of all the journalists who had worked for the newspaper during the occupation, including Hergé. On 26 September 1946, the story continued, restarting where it had been left off, in the first issue of the newly-created weekly magazine *Le Journal de Tintin*, under the title *Le Temple du Soleil* (*The Temple of the Sun*). It ran for 75 issues in the form of a double-page colour insert, with three double-width strips, sometimes including an educational text insert about the history of the Incas.

The story was then collected into two books by Casterman, the first with additional backgrounds by Edgar P Jacobs, the second involving a number of deletions and reformatting to fit into the four strips per single page/62-page book format.

Prior to running *The Seven Crystal Balls*, from 24 September to 12 November 1943, *Le Soir* presented *Dupont et Dupond Detectives* (*Thompson and Thomson Detectives*), 40 daily episodes of a narrative text serial – not comic strips – written by Paul Kinnet and illustrated by Hergé, that told the story of the Thompsons investigating a missing farmer. That story was never collected in book form.

Plot: Attending the music-hall at Moulinsart with Captain Haddock, Tintin renews his acquaintance with General Alcazar and learns in a dramatic fashion of the mysterious sleeping sickness which has struck one of the seven members of an archaeological expedition that brought back the Inca mummy, Rascar Capac. Two more archaeologists are struck soon after and the Thompsons come asking for Tintin's help. The only clues are small crystal fragments found near the victims. In spite of every precaution, three more archaeologists are struck, leaving only one, Prof. Hippolyte Bergamotte (Prof. Hercules Tarragon), an old friend of Prof. Calculus. Tintin, Haddock and Calculus spend the night at Tarragon's house, which is guarded by the police. They see the mummy, are the victims of strange phenomenon, such as an attack of ball lightning and a horrifying nightmare in which Rascar Capac appears, claiming his revenge. Tarragon is struck by an attacker who got into the house through the chimney. The police wound him but he escapes and, the next day, kidnaps Calculus who has unwittingly worn the mummy's sacred bracelet. A complex trail of clues, involving Alcazar's Peruvian helper, Chiquito, leads Tintin and Haddock to the French Atlantic harbour of La Rochelle, where they learn that their foes left for Peru with Calculus aboard the ship Pachacamac.

In Peru, Tintin and Haddock try to have the police board the Pachacamac but are foiled by a fake quarantine. Tintin sneaks aboard and finds Calculus. Chiquito tells him that the scientist will be sacrificed to the Sun God of the Incas. Tintin and Haddock follow the kidnappers' trail into the Andes in spite of an attempt on their lives. When Tintin helps a young local boy named Zorrino, his gesture is noticed by an Inca priest in disguise. A grateful Zorrino agrees to lead Tintin and Haddock to the Temple of the Sun, a secret mountain city ruled by the last Inca. After an arduous journey, they find a long-forgotten, hidden underground entrance into the Temple, but are later captured. In acknowledgement of Tintin's kindness to Zorrino, the Inca lets him choose the day and time when they will be burned at the stake, using magnified sunlight to set fire to a pyre. Tintin knowingly chooses the time of a forthcoming total eclipse. When the eclipse comes, the natives believe Tintin has the power to command the sun and release him. The Inca frees the seven archaeologists from their curse and lets Tintin and his friends go, having sworn to never reveal the Temple's existence.

Characters: The first book's most notable character is Professor Tarragon, a bombastic, exuberant scientist, who is to archaeology what Haddock is to the sea. Another interesting character is the archaeologist Marc Charlet (Mark Falconer), who looks like an older version of Tintin with dark hair. One regrets that their appearances are all too brief, and wonders what the adventures of Falconer and Tarragon would be like...

The second book, on the other hand, offers the memorable character of Zorrino, who is basically a Peruvian version of Tchang from *The Blue Lotus*, a younger version of Tintin, imbued with the ideals of bravery, friendship and loyalty that Hergé knew and remembered from his Scout years. The Inca is also a noble figure who appears to almost adopt Zorrino at the end, not unlike Wang Chen-Yee in the earlier book.

Continuity: The Seven Crystal Balls sees the return of General Alcazar, now in political exile, not seen since *Tintin and the Broken Ear*, and of Bianca Castafiore, the Milanese Nightingale, last suffered in *King Ottokar's Sceptre*. One of the cursed scientists is Professor Cantonneau, who accompanied Tintin in *The Shooting Star*.

Influences: In this arc, Hergé revisited the theme of the tragic curse that followed the discovery of King Tut's tomb by Howard Carter in 1922, which he had previously touched upon in *Cigars of the Pharaoh*. The theme of the discovery of a hidden Lost City is, of course, familiar to the readers of H Rider Haggard's *She* (1886) which inspired numerous literary descendants, the most famous being Edgar Rice Burroughs' La from *Tarzan and the Jewels of Opar* (1918). A more relevant French source, however, may be a novel by Gaston Leroux, the creator of Rouletabille, entitled *L'Épouse du Soleil* (*The Bride of the Sun*, 1913), which also deals with a hidden Inca city.

Trivia: The map of South America used and redrawn by Hergé on the first page of *Prisoners of the Sun* shows the northern part of Peru as belonging to its neighbour, Ecuador. This is a disputed area between the two countries and, as a result, the book was forbidden in Peru.

When *Prisoners of the Sun* was modified to fit into the standard Casterman book format, in addition to a general reformatting of the art (cropping, flipping etc.), a number of scenes were deleted for reasons of length. Among these are: a scene where Tintin chases away a cat aboard the Pachacamac (between pages 6 and 7 of the book version), various antics of the Thompsons (page 11), Haddock drawing a picture of Tintin on a wall (page 12), Haddock chewing some coca given to him by Zorrino to gain strength during their arduous mountain trek (page 22), Tintin shooting a jaguar (page 37) and Haddock coming across gold nuggets under the Temple of the Sun but being forced to leave them behind (page 44).

Over the years, many people have commented upon the fact that the eclipse of the sun shown on pages 58 and 59 moves in the right direction for the Southern hemisphere. (There was, in fact, a total eclipse over Peru on 25 January 1944.) What is puzzling is that the eclipse was drawn correctly in the original version published in Tintin, and the error was made during the reformatting of the story for book publication. One may be surprised that the Incas, whose priests were themselves astronomers, were unaware of the forthcoming eclipse, and further note that such an eclipse usually lasts up to three hours from beginning to end, not mere minutes as implied in the book.

Review: The Temple of the Sun arc represents one more leap forward in Hergé's graphic and narrative skills. This is due to the transition from daily black & white strips to full colour double pages, and is particularly evident in the lush scenes of the trek through the Andes in the second book. One should also take note of Tintin's remarkably surreal nightmare on page 23 of book two.

This time, Tintin does not seek a treasure but something infinitely more precious: the life of one of his dearest friends, Prof. Calculus. The stakes are therefore far more serious than those in the preceding series and the story is more captivating as a result.

The first book is bathed in the type of surreal atmosphere that Hergé knew how to create so well. The once discarded scene of the Arumbaya Indian appearing in Tintin's bedroom in a nightmare from *The Broken Ear* returns in an even more terrifying context, this time depicting the hideous mummy of Rascar Capac. The mysterious and seemingly unstoppable curse which strikes each of the archaeologists in turn is only revealed to have a human agent on page 37 – until then, Tintin faces his most shadowy and unfathomable foe. From the very first page, with his mysterious prophetic warning until that moment, Tintin is confronted with a dark and oppressive force, culminating with the night scenes inside Prof. Tarragon's house, that are worthy of a Hammer film.

The book then switches to the Hitchcockian thriller mode that Hergé had also mastered in the past. But in this instance, Tintin loses. He and Haddock cannot stop Prof. Calculus's kidnappers, and are condemned to play catch-up with them until the very end.

The second book offers a prodigious journey through the Andes, which involves confrontation with fears and inner demons, trials by fire and water, and self-sacrifice. Tintin risking his life to rescue Snowy and Zorrino, Haddock having to abandon the gold he so much desires; all of this makes the journey to the Temple of the Sun unforgettable. Perhaps, on a symbolic level, it is no coincidence that Tintin and his friends enter the Temple through a tomb, from death being reborn into life.

That sense of enlightenment is particularly on display in Tintin, who, in spite of his faith in his foreknowledge of the eclipse, evidences a state of Zen-like serenity that is simply unheard of among adventure heroes. Contrast this with the Thompsons' haphazard quest for their friends in every corner of the world, and the book becomes a philosophical parable, perhaps a hidden reflection of Hergé's spiritual yearnings, anticipating *Tintin In Tibet*. Both books: 5/5.

Land of Black Gold

Publishing History:

1. First version (58 black & white pages, uncompleted): serialisation in Belgium in *Le Petit Vingtième* from 25 September 1939, interrupted on 8 May 1940; serialisation in France in *Coeurs Vaillants–Âmes Vaillantes* from 4 August 1940, interrupted, then restarted in *Message aux Coeurs Vaillants* in June 1945, and in *Tintin et Milou*, ten issues from December 1945 to May 1946, under the title *Tintin et Milou au Pays de L'Or Liquide* (*Tintin and Snowy In the Land of Liquid Gold*).

2. Second version: serialisation in the Belgian edition of *Le Journal de Tintin* from 16 September 1948; and in the French edition of *Le Journal de Tintin* from 28 October 1948 (Nos. 1–44, 60–76).

3. *Tintin au Pays de L'Or Noir*, 62 pages, colour, Editions Casterman, Tournai, 1950.

4. *Tintin au Pays de L'Or Noir*, modernised redrawn version (with Bob De Moor), 62 pages, colour, Editions Casterman, Tournai, 1971.

As mentioned in *The Crab with the Golden Claws*, *Land of Black Gold* had initially run for 58 pages in *Le Petit Vingtième* from 28 September 1939 to 8 May 1940. On 9 May 1940, as a result of the Nazi invasion of Belgium, *Le Vingtième Siècle* and its weekly children's supplement were discontinued and *Land of Black Gold* was left uncompleted, at a point which roughly corresponds to page 30 of the current edition. These 58 black & white

desert. Meanwhile, the Thompsons, who have followed him, are also on his trail. Tintin finds water in time, then is witness to the sabotage of a pipeline by his old enemy, Dr Muller. They fight, but Muller escapes, stranding Tintin in the desert again. He is rescued by the Thompsons, and they eventually reach the capital of the local emirate. There, Tintin meets Emir Ben Kalish Ezab and learns that Muller (who poses as an archaeologist) is trying to force the Emir to sell his country's oil rights to competitors of his current western partners. Bab El Ehr is blamed for the rash of sabotage. Abdallah (Abdullah), the Emir's spoiled, bratty son, an incorrigible prankster, is kidnapped by Muller to put more pressure on the Emir. Tintin, with the help of his old friend, Portuguese merchant Oliveira da Figueira, infiltrates Muller's mountain citadel. He eventually succeeds in freeing Abdullah, but Muller and his men corner him. Tintin is rescued in the nick of time by Captain Haddock, while Muller escapes in a car with Abdullah. Tintin and Haddock pursue him and, thanks to Abdullah's pranks, capture him. The Thompsons accidentally find pills dropped by Muller and mistake them for aspirin, when they are in fact the secret compound that caused the gasoline to explode. They begin exhibiting strange symptoms of uncontrollable, multi-coloured hair growth. Muller is revealed to have been the agent of an unnamed foreign power trying to gain control of the Middle East and weaken the West.

Characters: The character who indisputably steals the show is Abdullah, the Emir's incredibly obnoxious child who makes Dennis the Menace look like a little angel.

(The character was reportedly suggested by Jacques Van Melkebeke.) When Hergé depicts the grieving Caliph showing his kidnapped son's portrait to Tintin, he notes that 'the artist [who painted it] went insane,' leaving the rest to our imagination. That's all the introduction we need. Abdullah more than fulfils his promise when we finally meet him. He is possibly the only character to have ever succeeded in driving Tintin so batty that he loses his cool. That Abdullah eventually discovers a love-hate relationship with Haddock – whom he calls 'Blistering-Barnacles' is almost a foregone conclusion.

Continuity: Dr Muller, last seen in *The Black Island*, returns and one must assume that his Soviet paymasters – the lead villain in *The Black Island* bore a Russian-sounding patronym – sprang him out of the jail where he was heading at the end of that book. By the end of the book, one almost feels sympathy for Muller, when he is subjected to Abdullah's pranks.

By the third version of *Land of Black Gold*, Hergé created the fictional Emirate of Khemed and the city of Wadesdah to serve as a background for Tintin's future middle-eastern adventure, *The Red Sea Sharks*. He further brought in the characters of Portuguese merchant Oliveira da Figueira and (in *The Red Sea Sharks* only) Sheikh Patrash Pasha from *Cigars of the Pharaoh*. Bianca Castafiore appears in a cameo on the radio. No one is safe from her, anywhere.

Influences: Initially, one can see how *Land of Black Gold* with its clear concern about war and rumours of war fit well immediately after *King Ottokar's Sceptre*, which also dealt with the rise of fascism. Hergé retained that pre-World War Two atmosphere in the first colour version, and the John Buchan, TE Lawrence of Arabia aspects of the story work better in that context. Yet, the third version of the book is better, because it incorporates the growing passion for exotic spy thrillers that began to sweep Western Europe in the 1950s with James Bond and his imitators. In many respects, in *Land of Black Gold* Hergé had anticipated the espionage novel of the next few decades.

Trivia: As we mentioned, the first black & white version stopped when Tintin is about to be caught in a sandstorm after his battle with Muller – a mix of scenes from pages 28 and 30 of the current version. Other changes included: the addition of Haddock, dispatched on a secret mission on page 3; Tintin making a divining rod to find first oil, then water, when he is stranded in the desert; Tintin being shown replacing Muller's henchman (page 25); and a general reorganisation of the Thompsons' funny antics in the desert, now shown to be driving a red jeep.

The changes between the first and coloured versions are far more substantial. Virtually everything between pages 6 and 26 has been redrawn à la *Black Island* by Bob De Moor, starting with the harbour scenes, the Speedol ship and especially the first Middle East scenes. Tintin no longer arrives in Haifa in British-occupied Palestine, is no longer arrested by British soldiers and is no longer kidnapped by the Irgun who have mistaken him for one of theirs (Finkelstein in the first version, Goldstein in the second), before being taken to Bab El Ehr. Now, Tintin arrives in Khemed, is arrested by regular Arab military and is kidnapped by, and taken directly to, Bab El Ehr. At that point, the pages are rearranged to accommodate the Thompsons' antics, which have not been substantially modified. In the first version, for example, the scene where they fall asleep at the wheel and crash into a mosque (page 34) took place earlier, without Tintin.

Review: Land of Black Gold suffers from its 'rebaked' nature, from both a story and graphic point of view; the book is pulled between the 'old' pre-war Tintin and the more modern one. Captain Haddock is retroactively shoe-horned into the story and Hergé, unable to come up with a plausible reason for his presence, uses it to his advantage to make fun of that fact, anticipating the self-referential and second-degree humour of *The Castafiore Emerald*.

There are some memorable moments in *Land of Black Gold* – all in the second half of the book. The character of Abdullah, as pointed out earlier, is a gem and the extraordinarily surreal symptoms of the Thompsons following the ingestion of Formula 14 is visually inspired. Hergé has lost none of his touch when it comes to creating unforgettable images. Somehow, there was a story with greater potential underneath the various elements, but Hergé was not able, or willing, to get it out. 2/5.

Destination Moon
Explorers on the Moon

Publishing History:

1. Serialisation in Belgium in *Le Journal de Tintin* from 30 March 1950, and in France in *Le Journal de Tintin* from 11 May 1950 (Nos. 82–105, 187–277).
2. *Objectif Lune*, 62 pages, colour, Editions Casterman, Tournai, 1953.
3. *On a Marché Sur la Lune*, 62 pages, colour, Editions Casterman, Tournai, 1954.

Even though Hergé had already toyed with the notion of sending Tintin to the Moon in the 1940s, had discussed such a story with Jacques Van Melkebeke and Dr Bernard Heveulmans, and had even started working on a couple of pages and an outline, the actual *Moon* story arc first appeared in serial form in *Le Journal de Tintin* under the overall title *On a Marché Sur la Lune* (*They Walked on the Moon*) in 1950. It continued until 1954, with an 18–month interruption for health reasons after only two dozen pages had been published.

The story was then collected into two books by Casterman, with the usual deletions for reasons of space, and some minor recolouring and reformatting, in 1953 and 1954.

Plot: Upon returning to Marlinspike, Tintin and Haddock are summoned to Syldavia by Prof. Calculus. There, they find him working at a vast atomic research centre, planning a nuclear-powered rocket trip to the

Moon. Naturally, he wants Tintin and Haddock to join him and his assistant, Engineer Wolff. He introduces them to Mr Baxter, the head of the Centre. But Calculus's rocket is coveted by an unidentified rival power who succeed in placing a mole at the Centre. The Thompsons arrive. Information leaks out and a rocket prototype is almost hijacked by the enemy but, thanks to Tintin's forethought, it is destroyed in flight. Later, following an argument with Haddock, Calculus suffers a bout of amnesia but is cured. Eventually, the time of departure arrives and the rocket takes off, but not before the enemy has managed to sneak Tintin's old foe, Boris Jorgen, on board.

Calculus's rocket is en route to the Moon with Calculus, Wolff, Tintin, Haddock… and the Thompsons who mistook the time of departure. Haddock has one drink too many and goes on a space walk which could strand him in outer space if not for Tintin's daring rescue. The Thompsons' colourful hair syndrome resurfaces. They eventually land on the Moon. Tintin is the first man to walk on our satellite. They explore the surface in a tank-like vehicle and Tintin discovers ice beneath the surface when he rescues Snowy, who fell into a crevice. Eventually, Jorgen comes out of hiding and Wolff is revealed as the mole. Jorgen takes Tintin prisoner and tries to take off, abandoning Calculus, Haddock and the Thompsons. Tintin frees himself in the nick of time and captures him. During their return to Earth, Jorgen escapes but is shot in a struggle with Wolff. Aware that there is not enough oxygen for all the passengers, Wolff throws himself into space. The rocket barely manages to make it back to Earth and its passengers are successfully reanimated.

Characters: The *Moon* story belongs to Prof. Calculus, as *Red Rackham's Treasure* belonged to Haddock. Yes, it is Tintin who repeatedly saves the day but, from beginning to end, it is Calculus's cosmic vision that moves the story forward. When he becomes incapacitated, Mission Chief Baxter agonisingly tells the doctors that without Calculus there can be no moon journey, and he is right. Calculus has many fine moments in the book: his righteous wrath when called a 'goat' by the Captain; his self-doubts before the launch; his fear – greater than that of death! – that his calculations may be wrong when about to face a meteor; his trust in Wolff against overwhelming evidence; and his final, visionary speech in which he promises that, one day, men shall return to the Moon.

The other memorable character is Wolff, the meek, supposedly devoted and loyal engineer, who turns out to be a traitor, not because of any political convictions or an evil nature but because he is being blackmailed over gambling debts. The weak-willed Wolff eventually redeems himself and saves his colleagues through an act of supreme sacrifice. Wolff is a unique character in the *Tintin* gallery, someone who was not what we initially thought, and who, in the end, we wish we could have known better. Wolff would not be out of place in a John Le Carré novel.

Continuity: This is Syldavia's finest hour! The Ruritania-like country introduced in *King Ottokar's Sceptre* is suddenly able to mount man's first expedition into outer space – although it is hinted that this is an international effort and the space centre's boss is named Baxter after all. In an earlier version of the story, Prof. Phostle from *The Shooting Star* was intended to be part of the team.

Conversely, if it is unclear who the true villains are – Hergé is here reusing the same storytelling device as in *The Shooting Star* of showing mostly reaction shots of Tintin's foes – we know that their agent is the same renegade Syldavian colonel, Boris Jorgen, last seen in *King Ottokar's Sceptre*.

The comical effect of the Thompsons' multicoloured hair growth introduced at the end of *Land of Black Gold* is well utilised here for comic effect.

Influences: In a 1933 panel of his *Quick & Flupke* series, Hergé had drawn a poster showing the smiling Moon face that was also used by filmmaker Georges Mélies in his 1902 *A Trip to the Moon*, itself loosely based on Jules Verne's famous 1865 novel, *From the Earth to the Moon*, and its 1870 sequel, *Around the Moon*. The cover of the 1950 issue of *Le Journal de Tintin*, heralding the start of *On a Marché Sur la Lune*, also featured the same Moon face with Tintin and his friends shown walking on our satellite. The connection between Hergé's story and Verne's, direct or indirect, is therefore well established.

There are more than a few similarities between Verne's *Around the Moon* and Hergé's book, including verbatim lines of dialogue in the countdown scene (Chapter I of the novel), most of the space antics, the discovery of water on the moon (Chapter XVII) and the desperate finalé (Chapter XXII). Again, Jacques Van Melkebeke's contribution in helping Hergé shape the story was presumably the source of these similarities.

It is also likely that the film *Destination Moon*, shot in 1949 and 1950, and based on Robert Heinlein's *Rocketship Galileo* (1947), was also an influence. Hergé himself credited astronautics professor Alexander Ananoff, who was even shown a model of the Moon Rocket. Finally, Leslie Simon's book, *German Research In World War II*, shown on page 23 of *The Calculus Affair*, a real book published in 1947 by J Wily & Sons in New York, shows on its cover a V-2 rocket with the same red & white checker motif as Tintin's.

Trivia: In the earlier draft, Hergé had decided to locate the Moon Project in the fictional American locale of Radio City. Curiously, the only time the chief villain is named is when he identifies himself by the Anglo-Saxon name of "Miller" to his minister on page 54 of *Destination Moon*. Could the British (Americans don't have ministers) be behind the skulduggery?

Changes made between the version serialised in *Le Journal de Tintin* and that collected in book form included a recolouring (the original uniforms were all green) and the deletion of some sequences, such as one showing Snowy almost being dumped in space bundled with the Thompsons' hair, and a longer sequence on the Moon showing the Thompsons getting lost, almost running out of air, then suffering from oxygen-induced euphoria.

In 1969, the magazine *Paris-Match* (a French *Life*) – which Hergé later lampooned as *Paris-Flash* in *The*

Castafiore Emerald – asked Hergé to draw a realistic four-page sequence depicting the actual Apollo XII Moon journey and landing.

Review: The *Moon* story is Hergé at his best. The book is a triumphant achievement on virtually every level. Story-wise, the characters are pitched perfectly and, as mentioned above, Wolff rises to true literature level. The suspense is carefully maintained, first in an espionage context – who is the mole? how can the heroes thwart the saboteurs? – then in outer space. The sense of uncertainty is very real before the rocket launch and at every step of the journey. The characters – and we – do not doubt that they could die, which is quite a feat in a comic book series!

Hergé uses a lot of scientific exposition but always counterpoints it with some humorous elements, such as Haddock's remarks. The wonders of the journey into space and the exploration of the Moon always reflect this multi-layered story structure: the dry, scientific elements are perfectly balanced against the humanity, and in the case of the Thompsons, the humorous antics of the characters.

Hergé wisely resisted the impulse to show Selenites or any other outer space creatures. Like Verne, he establishes the presence of water on the Moon and during Tintin's rescue of Snowy from the lunar underground we are left to wonder what else may lie hidden deep inside the surface. The 'sense of wonder' so dear to the classic science fiction writers is present here in abundance.

Then we come to the ending. Tintin and his friends'

JEAN-MARC AND RANDY LOFFICIER

perilous journey back to Earth takes place at a hell-
bent pace, always with one more danger to overcome.
This is a roller-coaster ride. The book almost ends too
soon, with its Disney-like final twist of making us
believably fear for Haddock's life.

Graphically, and taking into account the science of
the times (no photos of the Earth seen from space
existed back then), the book has withstood the test of
time better than most other proto-space exploration
novels. Hergé's clean and detailed line is at the peak of
its form, and particularly suits the mood of this book:
the science halls of the space centre as well as the bleak
lunar landscape. *Explorers on the Moon* is a true epic of
the human imagination. Both books: 5/5.

The Calculus Affair

Publishing History:
1. Serialisation in Belgium in *Le Journal de Tintin* from
   December 1954, and in France in *Le Journal de Tintin*
   from February 1955 (Nos. 328–389).
2. *L'Affaire Tournesol*, 62 pages, colour, Editions
   Casterman, Tournai, 1956.

Plot: During a storm, obnoxious insurance salesman
Seraphin Lampion (Jolyon Wagg) finds refuge at
Marlinspike and witnesses a series of inexplicable glass-
shattering incidents. Later, strangers are found lurking
in the Castle's grounds shooting at each other. Calculus
leaves for Geneva; Tintin notices that the glass-shat-
tering stopped after his departure and visits his labora-

tory, where he discovers a Bordurian spy, who escapes. Tintin and Haddock follow Calculus to Switzerland and, in spite of the Bordurians' attempts to stop them, make contact with Calculus's colleague, Prof. Topolino, who reveals that their friend was working on a deadly, destructive ultrasonic device. Tintin and Haddock find out that Calculus was kidnapped by the Bordurians and try to free him; instead, the scientist is taken by Syldavian operatives. A long chase ensues by helicopter and then by car, but they fail to stop the Syldavians from taking off in a small plane with Calculus. They later learn that the plane was shot down over Borduria. Tintin and Haddock travel to Borduria but are put under surveillance by the secret police. They escape and, thanks to Bianca Castafiore's providential help, they manage to steal Red Cross passes signed by Secret Police chief Colonel Sponz, that enable them to spring Calculus out of the fortress where he was kept prisoner. A fierce pursuit ensues, during which Tintin steals a tank from the Bordurians. They eventually make it to the border. Calculus destroys the microfilms of his weapon's schematics, which were kept in his umbrella all the time.

Characters: The introduction of Jolyon Wagg and, to a lesser degree, of the Cutts' butcher shop, marks yet another turning point in the series. Wagg is loud, obnoxious, intrusive, overbearing and ever unaware of not being wanted or appreciated. From the very beginning of *The Calculus Affair*, to its bitter end where he and his family have taken to squatting in Marlinspike, he is a recurring obstacle, one more hurdle thrown in the Captain's life by a merciless fate, just to make his life miserable. Yet, Wagg (unlike earlier comical characters) is not a mere one-dimensional stereotype. He is a fully fleshed-out individual of a type that is, sadly, known to us all. Hergé engages here in bitter and successful social satire.

Continuity: After Syldavia in the previous book, we now get a chance to focus on its old rival, Borduria. In *King Ottokar's Sceptre*, Borduria stood in for Nazi Germany. In *The Calculus Affair*, it stands in for Cold War Russia or Ceaucescu's Romania. Its moustachioed dictator, Pleksy-Gladz (Kurvi-Tasch), is reminiscent of Stalin; its police state, well represented by the evil Colonel Sponz (who returned in *Tintin and the Picaros*), is a convincing KGB analogue.

The Moon expedition is referred to several times in the story: Tintin is welcomed in Borduria as the first man to walk on the Moon and he later remarks that he has not driven a tank since the Moon. Yet, one is puzzled that the Syldavia (presumably) of King Muskar XII, which decorated Tintin in *King Ottokar's Sceptre*, and later welcomed Calculus and an international community of scientists to launch the heroic and peaceful Moon project, is now portrayed as a criminal state capable of threatening Tintin and violently kidnapping Calculus – as if he had to be forced to return to Syldavia! This sudden change in Syldavian methods and politics is unexplained, is not in continuity and ultimately strains believability.

The Castafiore returns in a superb performance where she shows that behind her dizzy appearance is a clever mind at work. The wily way in which she handles Sponz is a model, yet unrehearsed, performance. This is perhaps her finest appearance in the entire series.

Influences: 1954 was the height of the Cold War and the popularity of espionage thrillers in France and Belgium was at its peak – entire book imprints were devoted to the exploits of not only James Bond, but an entire army of home-grown secret agents, such as OSS 117 or Francis Coplan FX-18. It was only natural that Tintin followed in their footsteps and became engaged in rescuing a scientist kidnapped behind the Iron Curtain.

Trivia: Leslie Simon's book, *German Research In World War II*, shown on page 23, with its interior illustration, which provides the 'MacGuffin' of *The Calculus Affair*, is a real book, published in 1947 by J Wily & Sons in New York. (There is also a 1948 British edition by Chapman & Hall.) There is only one small change: on the actual book cover, the plane silhouette is inscribed with a swastika, which Hergé eliminated when he redrew it...

The presence of this book raises an interesting point because it is almost the only time in the *Tintin* series that World War Two is ever referred to. In fact, one wonders when such a war could have taken place, if it did at all, since war was obviously averted in *Land of Black Gold* and none of the subsequent events leave any room for a World War. This is yet one more factor that somehow clashes with the coherence of the *Tintin* universe as it had been carefully built until then.

Review: Graphically, *The Calculus Affair* is when Hergé's preoccupation with ultra-realistic backgrounds and props reached its peak, even more so than in the *Moon* books, whose contents heavily drew upon the author's imagination. The book was prepared almost as a film, with real 'location' scouting being done around Geneva. Studio assistants were instructed to draw highly realistic details of cars, planes, whatever mechanical or real-life elements were needed for a panel on a piece of tracing paper that was later incorporated in the finished art. This was the first book where Hergé pencilled his pages separately from the finished, inked artwork in order to better control the assembling of disparate elements.

Story-wise, Hergé is trying to do the Cold War and the action part of the story indeed works remarkably well as a spy thriller on a superficial level. However, the plot seems somewhat shoe-horned into the familiar universe and stretches believability. First and foremost, one wonders why Calculus would willingly work on such a potentially destructive device. Certainly, the Calculus from *Destination Moon* who described the focus of his research as exclusively humanitarian and was concerned about 'protecting mankind from new methods of destruction', hardly seems the logical candidate to design such a deadly device. The ending is similarly unconvincing: burning a microfilm will hardly prevent the villains from reverse engineering Calculus' device. This, after all, is not a secret chemical formula. Lastly, it is impossible to believe that Syldavia would stoop to sending agents to hurt Tintin and kidnap Calculus, not after everything that occurred before.

Ultimately, one feels that Hergé's heart was not really

much into the action part of the story. The espionage plot is an excuse to focus on the comical, or rather satirical, elements of the tale. *The Calculus Affair* is filled with self-derision: Jolyon Wagg is our heroes' true nemesis, not the Bordurians, who are mostly clowns with ineffective weapons. The car chase of Calculus's kidnappers is Hitchcockian and most dramatic in *The Seven Crystal Balls*; here, it is but a pretext for a series of jokes involving a manic Italian driver, a Swiss gendarme who is an exact lookalike of the Thompsons (are all idiot policemen in Hergé's universe of Thompson clones?) and a wonderful village scene that seems almost lifted from popular French humour artist Dubout. Hergé seems to rejoice more in having invented his classic Band-Aid gag – which was reused in later books – than in creating a believable threat.

The Calculus Affair is a faux thriller in the same way that *The Castafiore Emerald* – which it anticipates – is a faux detective novel. 3/5.

The Red Sea Sharks

Publishing History:
1. Serialisation in Belgium in *Le Journal de Tintin* from October 1956, and in France in *Le Journal de Tintin* from December 1956 (Nos. 425–486).
2. *Coke en Stock*, 62 pages, colour, Editions Casterman, Tournai, 1958.

As Hergé became older, and Tintin's success grew by leaps and bounds – by then, the sales of a new book totalled nearly half-a-million, from a little under 100,000 before the war – the time elapsed between each successive book began to grow longer as well. The original French title *Coke En Stock* refers to the coded message used by the slavers to indicate the presence of a cargo of slaves onboard a ship.

Plot: Tintin and Haddock accidentally bump into General Alcazar. Meanwhile, Khemed Emir Ben Kalish Ezab has been overthrown by rival Sheikh Bab El Ehr and has sent his bratty son Abdullah to stay at Marlinspike. Thanks to the Thompsons' unwitting help, Tintin discovers that Alcazar has been buying fighter planes from his old foe, Dawson. The same type of planes are also responsible for Bab El Ehr's victory. Dawson discovers Tintin's snooping; when the young reporter and Haddock fly to Khemed, he arranges for a bomb to be placed on board. Tintin and Haddock escape and, thanks to Senhor Oliveira Da Figueira's help, manage to reach the Emir's hiding place. There they learn that the coup was financed and armed by mysterious billionaire Di Gorgonzola, who is also involved in the gun-running and slave trade. On their way out of Khemed, Tintin's boat is attacked by Bab El Ehr's planes; he and Haddock become stranded at sea on a raft with Piotr Szut (Skut), one of the downed planes' pilots. They are picked up by Di Gorgonzola's cruise ship – the villain is now revealed to be Rastapopoulos in disguise – then handed over to the steamer Ramona, captained by the nefarious Allan. On Rastapopoulos' orders, Allan sets the Ramona on fire then abandons the ship. Tintin and

Haddock succeed in putting out the fire and free the African slaves who were kept prisoner aboard. Rastapopoulos orders his pirate submarine to sink the Ramona. Haddock and his African crew manage to avoid the torpedoes until Tintin can successfully radio a US battleship for help. Rastapopoulos escapes arrest by fleeing in a pocket submarine. His ring is dismantled. Abdullah returns home but Haddock is now plagued by Jolyon Wagg.

Characters: There are so many old characters crowding each other in *The Red Sea Sharks* that there is hardly any room left to develop new ones. Piotr Skut, the basically decent and loyal pilot of one of Bab El Ehr's plane shot down by Tintin, is a nice supporting character, but nothing more. There is hardly even any room for Prof. Calculus and the Thompsons.

Continuity: The Red Sea Sharks is virtually a sequel to *Land of Black Gold*; we again meet Emir Ben Kalish Ezab, his prankster son Abdullah, perennial rival Bab El Ehr and the wonderful Senhor Oliveira Da Figueira. Added to the mix is the unseen but mentioned Sheikh Patrash Pasha from *Cigars of the Pharaoh.* Also present is the evil Dr Muller from *The Black Island*, now rechristened 'Mull Pasha,' in charge of Bab El Ehr's defence.

The Red Sea Sharks is otherwise a true continuity feast, heralding the return of Rastapopoulos, unseen since *The Blue Lotus*, now returning disguised as Mephistopheles (!) and teamed up with the evil Captain Allan (last seen in *The Crab with Golden Claws*), General Alcazar (last seen in *The Seven Crystal Balls*) and former Shanghai Chief of Police, Dawson (also from *The Blue Lotus*).

Last but not least, the Castafiore has a cameo and Jolyon Wagg returns at the end to make the Captain's life more miserable after Abdullah's departure.

Influences: Hergé reportedly embarked on *The Red Sea Sharks* after reading a newspaper article dealing with the issue of slavery in the Middle East. The book offered him an opportunity to revisit themes that he had already touched upon in *Cigars of the Pharaoh*, *Tintin and the Broken Ear* and, of course, *Land of Black Gold*.

Trivia: Initially, the dialogue of the African slaves was written in very bad French, which was hardly surprising since these are clearly poor people, speaking in a foreign language. After this aspect of the story was labelled racist by the African magazine *Jeune Afrique*, Hergé rewrote the text in a 1967 reprinting in conversant French, conveying some phonetic flavour through the suppression of the occasional letter.

Review: The Red Sea Sharks is very effective as a modern political thriller and far more believable than *The Calculus Affair*. In fact, it has virtually not aged – unfortunately, there are still reports of slavery coming out of that area of the world.

Harking back to *Tintin*'s early days, it seems torn from the headlines. Hergé has lost none of his touch when it comes to dramatising the dirty business of the world. Gun-running, drug-smuggling, coups and counter-coups, and now the slave trade – *The Red Sea Sharks* reads almost as a compendium of Hergé's political ideas.

The political analysis may, in fact, be more profound that even its author intended. Take, for instance, the character of Emir Ben Kalish Ezab of Khemed. One wonders why the reader should feel any sympathy towards him: it is clear that the man is a self-centred autocrat, no better than Bab El Ehr, who cares more for his pet leopard than for his men. The story makes it clear that he had turned a blind eye towards the slave trade until the villains refused one of Abdullah's most ludicrous requests. Is he supposed to be on our side merely because he sells his oil to us? Is restoring him to power the happy ending that the book suggests – other than ridding Marlinspike of Abdullah? The whole dynamic of the western world's dealings with the Arab world is appropriately captured, if not resolved, in *The Red Sea Sharks*.

The scenes pitting Rastapopoulos' submarine against the Ramona are superbly choreographed. For a comic book to tackle the concept of such a battle so well would have been inconceivable for any artist but Hergé.

The Red Sea Sharks is a fan favourite because of the gamut of old characters that cross paths (or almost do) in the book. It is almost as if Hergé was doing some house-cleaning of his past works and characters before embarking on something more serious and with more personal resonance. 4/5.

Tintin In Tibet

Publishing History:
1. Serialisation in Belgium in *Le Journal de Tintin* from September 1958, and in France in *Le Journal de Tintin* from October 1958 (Nos. 523–585).
2. *Tintin au Tibet*, 62 pages, colour, Editions Casterman, Tournai, 1960.

After *The Red Sea Sharks*, Hergé marked a pause. At that time, writer-artist Michel Greg was involved with the production of the *Tintin* animated television series, produced by Raymond Leblanc, publisher of *Le Journal de Tintin*. Hergé asked Greg for possible *Tintin* stories; two were written and partially developed, *Le Thermozéro* and *Les Pillules* (*The Pills*), both involving Tintin rescuing a secret agent and becoming involved with a 'cold bomb' in the first case, and some 'radioactive pills' in the latter. Hergé also toyed for a time with a remake of *Tintin In America*, and a story in which Captain Haddock's butler, Nestor, was framed for murder by his former employer, the Bird Brothers. The story that Hergé eventually decided to tell was an adventure that took Tintin to Tibet, which he initially entitled *Le Museau de la Vache* (*The Cow's Muzzle*) after a mountain peak in the Himalayas.

Plot: While on vacation in Switzerland, Tintin has a vivid dream of his friend Tchang surviving a plane crash; he then learns that Tchang's plane did crash in Tibet. Convinced of the truth of his dream, Tintin, followed by a sceptical Haddock, travels to Tibet. With the help of sherpa Tharkey they mount an expedition into the Himalayas and find the plane wreck. In an ice cave, Tintin discovers evidence that Tchang survived the crash but Tharkey still believes that the boy is dead, perhaps killed by the mysterious Yeti, whose trail they have crossed. Tharkey leaves. Undaunted, Tintin goes on, followed by Haddock. Tharkey, moved by Tintin's selflessness, returns just in time to save them during a perilous climb. After an avalanche, they are found by the lamas of Khor-Biyong. The vision of one of them, the supernaturally-gifted Blessed Lightning, leads Tintin further on the trail of Tchang, who is captive of the Yeti, whom the Tibetans call 'Migou.' Tintin eventually rescues Tchang, who tells him that the Yeti found him and fed him. The Yeti returns but is scared away by a flash from Tintin's camera. Tintin, Haddock and Tchang are honoured by the lamas and return home. The Yeti misses Tchang.

Characters: Tintin In Tibet is rich in finely drawn characters. Tharkey is a wonderful example of the loyal and trusted guide or companion to heroes whose archetype is well known to students of myth – or popular fiction. Gone are the stereotypes of the earlier *Tintin* books. Tharkey is as real as any character ever played by an actor on film.

The lamas of Khor-Biyong, in particular the Abbot and Blessed Lightning, are also well drawn; however, their representation is more conventional, fitting into the traditional perception of Tibetan lamas as wise men, occasionally capable of paranormal feats such as levitation, extrasensory perception etc. This concept was, of course, borrowed from Lobsang Rampa and other, not always trustworthy, sources.

Continuity: Tintin In Tibet marks the return of young Tchang Tchong-Jen, last seen in *The Blue Lotus*. At the time, Hergé had no evidence that he would later be able to renew his acquaintance with his real-life friend, who had left Belgium in 1935.

Influences: The original impetus for *Tintin In Tibet* was provided by a story commissioned from Jacques Van Melkebeke in 1954, just before he and Hergé broke up over a variety of personal issues. Van Melkebeke's project likely reused themes from his 1941 *Tintin* play, *M. Boullock a Disparu* (*The Disappearance of Mr Boullock*), in which Tintin had visited Tibet, and was further inspired by Maurice Herzog and Louis Lachenal's Anapurna climb of 1950, and Sir Edmund Hillary and Tenzing's Everest climb of 1953.

After Hergé had decided on Tibet as his theme, he was reportedly influenced by *Sur la Piste des Bêtes Ignorées* (*On the Trail of Forgotten Beasts*), a book by his friend Bernard Heuvermans which dealt with mythical animals, among them the Yeti or Abominable Snowman. Hergé later met Herzog, who claimed to have personally seen Yeti trails in Tibet.

Finally, the desire to do a book about Tibet was undoubtedly shaped by Hergé's increasing attraction towards oriental philosophies such as Buddhism and Taoism. Hergé's personal spiritual yearnings combined with the breakdown of his first marriage and the new relationship with his future second wife, to create a troubled period in his life, punctuated by disturbing dreams. This led him to undergo psychoanalysis with Professor Ricklin, a student of Carl Jung. For the more exotic, or paranormal aspect of Tibetan culture, Hergé relied on the works by Alexandra David-Neel[1] and, unfortunately, on *The Third Eye* (1956, translated into French in 1957) by the so-called T Lobsang Rampa.[2]

Trivia: The notion of ultimately making the Yeti a sympathetic character, as evidenced by Tchang's remark pitying his captor, reportedly originated with Fanny Vlamynck, who later became Hergé's second wife.

A sequence in which Tintin's stove almost explodes was cut out of the book version for reasons of length.

Review: Tintin In Tibet was Hergé's favourite *Tintin* book, certainly the most personal, which reflected not only his philosophical aspirations but also the personal drama which he lived at the time. The moving scene in which Captain Haddock proposes to sacrifice himself in order to not be responsible for Tintin's death as well, when he states that one victim is better than two, is a

[1] Alexandra David-Neel (1868–1969) was a Buddhist, an explorer, an author and a feminist; she was the first European woman to explore the forbidden city of Lhasa.

[2] 'Tuesday Lobsang Rampa' (-1981) claimed to have been born into a wealthy Tibetan family and to have studied in Lhasa to become a lama, and then to have undergone an operation that opened up the 'third eye' in the middle of his forehead, thus giving him psychic powers. A group of Tibetan scholars in Britain hired a detective, Clifford Burgess, to determine whether or not Rampa's story was true. Burgess discovered that Rampa had never been to Tibet, nor had he had any operation done to his forehead. Instead Rampa was actually Cyril Henry Hoskins, born in Devon, England, and son of a plumber named Joseph Henry Hoskins.

conscious or unconscious reflection of the pain felt by Hergé over the break-up of his first marriage.

Tintin In Tibet is also arguably the best book in the series; it was, in fact, voted the best French-language graphic novel ever done in an Internet poll of professionals, editors and critics. The reasons for that are easy to see: the book reaches a degree of perfection, both in its story and its stunning art, that has rarely been equalled, before or since.

Tintin In Tibet is the ultimate *Tintin* novel, in that it embodies both the thrill of adventure and the deep humanity of the characters. The 'MacGuffin' here is not a fetish, a sceptre, a lost treasure or a secret formula, but the life of a friend. By persevering against all odds, Tintin at last becomes the living embodiment of those virtues Hergé tried to honour out of the scouting experiences of his youth when he launched the series.

One would have to have a heart of stone not to be moved by the many effective emotional moments that punctuate the book: Haddock's grudging but ultimately constant support; his attempt to sacrifice himself to save Tintin's life; Tharkey's return; the discovery of the starving Tchang; the reverence of the lamas before Tintin; and ultimately the pathos of the Yeti having lost his only friend. For a comic book to handle such powerful emotions, convey them to the readers and make them feel what the characters are feeling, is a rare and precious achievement.

A mere comparison between the colourful pulp serial Fakirs from *Cigars of the Pharaoh* and *The Blue Lotus* and the wise lamas of Khor-Biyong is enough to measure the phenomenal distance travelled by Hergé in his approach to storytelling. With *Tintin In Tibet*, Tintin leaves the four-colour dime serial area to enter classic literature.

Visually, Hergé's mastery of space and details has never been so stunning. From its unforgettable mountain scenes, with its white spaces delineated by a line that always achieves perfection, to the details of the Tibetan artefacts, *Tintin In Tibet* is a constant feast for the eyes. The surreal scene of Haddock's nightmare on page 16 ranks with the best of Dali and Chirico – which, considering Hergé's awareness of modern art, was probably not a coincidence. Even his Yeti, when finally revealed, does not disturb the willing suspension of disbelief that sometimes occurs when the monster is finally revealed.

Tintin In Tibet is, in many respects, not only the ultimate *Tintin* book, it is the last *Tintin* book. 5/5.

The Castafiore Emerald

Publishing History:
1. Serialisation in Belgium and in France in *Le Journal de Tintin* from July 1961 (Nos. 665–726).
2. *Les Bijoux de la Castafiore*, 62 pages, colour, Editions Casterman, Tournai, 1963.

Plot: In Marlinspike, Tintin and Haddock meet a gypsy tribe and invite them to stay on the Castle grounds. An old fortune-teller foresees trouble ahead. Indeed, a dismayed Haddock later learns of the Castafiore's impending arrival but twists his ankle on a broken step and is confined to a wheelchair before he has time to flee. The arrival of the diva – and her jewels – attracts the attention of the international press, both openly and through spies. Relying on mistaken information obtained from Prof. Calculus, who misheard the questions, journalists from *Paris-Flash* publish an article that announces the forthcoming wedding of Haddock and the Castafiore. Later, during the filming of a television appearance, the Castafiore's jewels are discovered to be missing, but it turns out that they have just been misplaced. However, soon after, an emerald disappears. The Thompsons investigate, suspecting everyone, before fixing their attention on the Gypsies. Tintin looks into the strange behaviour of the Castafiore's pianist, Igor Wagner, but it too proves to be a false lead. Eventually, Haddock gets back on his feet and the Castafiore leaves. Tintin discovers the real thief: a magpie, who had stolen other small, shiny things before. He recovers the missing emerald. Life returns to normal in Marlinspike, except that Haddock trips again on the broken step that had been repaired.

Characters: Centre stage is the Castafiore, who appears here as an indomitable force of nature, living in a world of her own making. She never gets the Captain's name right, she thinks Calculus went up in a balloon, she makes up the rules as she goes, changing them to fit her mercurial moods. With Hergé's typical attention to detail, her changes in wardrobe are impressive, with a new and superb dress introduced in every sequence.

The Godot-character of the story is Mr Bolt, the

Marlinspike handyman who is supposed to come and repair the broken step throughout the book but who, like someone out of *Fawlty Towers*, comes up with one lame and transparent lie after another not to show up – even though we see him at home, or playing in the local band. Without Bolt's *laissez-faire* attitude, many of the book's events would be radically altered, and that broken step is like a Greek God's curse that affects every character's life for the worst. All except the Castafiore, who seems almost magically unaffected by it.

Finally, one should take note of the parrot given as a gift by the Castafiore to Haddock. Far worse than those seen in *Tintin In the Congo* and *Tintin and the Broken Ear*, this is an evil beast, immediately identified by Snowy and the Castle's cat as an object of mistrust, whose sole purpose in life is to drive the Captain crazy. The one-panel nightmare in which Haddock sees himself naked at the Opera, sitting in an audience of identical parrots all looking disapprovingly at him, is a terrifying visual representation of the power of the parrot!

Continuity: Jean-Loup de la Batellerie (Christopher Willoughby-Drupe) and his photographer Marco Rizotto from *Paris-Flash*, a lampooning of the often inaccurate *Paris-Match*, are introduced here. They were retroactively inserted by Bob De Moor in *The Black Island* and returned in *Tintin and the Picaros*.

Jolyon Wagg makes a return appearance and finally meets his match in the Castafiore. We learn that Tchang is now a student in London. Captain Chester and

Senhor Oliveira Da Figueira are among those sending congratulatory telegrams to Haddock. The Moon journey is referred to by the journalists.

Influences: While Hergé denied any specific knowledge of the *Nouveau Roman* of the mid-50s and early 60s, one certainly feels that, after crafting the ultimate *Tintin* book with *Tintin In Tibet*, there was no alternative left to him other than to deconstruct his own myth and create the antithesis of a *Tintin* adventure, which he did with *The Castafiore Emerald*.

The *Nouveau Roman* questioned the traditional modes of literary realism. It is commonly associated with the works of Marguerite Duras, Alain Robbe-Grillet, Michel Butor and Nathalie Sarraute, and is characterised by an austere narrative tone, often eschewing metaphor in favour of precise physical descriptions, a heightened sense of ambiguity and self-reflexive commentary on the processes of literary composition. *The Castafiore Emerald* is Hergé's version of a *Nouveau Roman*.

Trivia: Hergé's lampooning of *Paris-Flash* was based on a previous encounter with the real-life *Paris-Match* which had featured an error-riddled article on Hergé and his publisher.

Review: *The Castafiore Emerald* is a comedy of errors, a wonderful tribute to Murphy's Law. Absolutely everything that can go wrong in the book does.

The characters all live under some kind of omnipotent curse, perhaps victims of the Castafiore who certainly is at the centre of it. The curse appears when she does and is lifted when she leaves. Can it be that, like an accursed goddess of chaos, she travels with a cloud of misery above and around her?

Poor Haddock is the curse's main victim: he is bitten twice, once by the gypsy girl, then by the parrot. He is crippled and condemned to spend the book in a wheelchair. He is painfully stung by a wasp, publicly humiliated and then married to his worst nightmare. He cannot even get the lowly Mr Bolt to come and fix his broken step.

None of the other characters fare any better: Calculus's colour television prototype is a nightmarish failure; after years of loyal service, Nestor is suspected of being a thief (a reminiscence of one of Hergé's discarded plots?); the Thompsons crash their car and lose the Emerald; even supporting characters like the Castafiore's entourage and the various media people are plagued by insects, animals and technical incidents. No one gets out of here intact.

It is not too far a stretch to notice that even material objects seem struck by the same curse: the Marlinspike telephone system – not always too efficient in the past – now sends every other call to Cutts; the Castle's broken step exacts its pound of pain from everyone who dares step on it; bad traffic causes the television people to be late; the car brakes fail the Thompsons; the wheelchair assaults Calculus and the Doctor etc.

Even Tintin seems more reactive than proactive; he tepidly follows one false lead after another. Failing to find any criminal mastermind or international ring of jewel thieves, he becomes almost despondent, almost useless – until his brilliant stroke of inspiration at the end.

Hergé claimed that, with *The Castafiore Emerald*, he wanted to craft a book 'about nothing.' On the contrary, the book is *Seinfeld*-like in its dissection of the myriad, seemingly insignificant, details of the daily life at Marlinspike, incidents which are, in fact, enormously important. *The Castafiore Emerald* is a visual illustration of the famous chaos theory, in which the flap of the wing of a butterfly is said to create storms on the other side of the world. The book's incredible density of minute details has been the subject of several serious articles and an entire book analysed it page by page.

The cover illustration of *The Castafiore Emerald* shows Tintin, smiling mischievously and looking straight at the reader, his index finger before his mouth in the universal hush sign. It sums up the book very well, and says to those who come in late, 'don't spoil the joke.' 4/5.

Flight 714

Publishing History:
1. Serialisation in Belgium and in France in *Le Journal de Tintin* from September 1966 (Nos. 836–997).
2. *Vol 714 Pour Sidney*, 62 pages, colour, Editions Casterman, Tournai, 1968.

Plot: En route for an astronautic congress in Sydney, Tintin, Haddock and Calculus meet their old friend Piotr Skut, who is now a pilot for misanthropic billionaire Laszlo Carreidas. Carreidas invites them to join him in his private plane and they accept. Later, the plane is hijacked by traitorous secretary Spalding and co-pilot Colombani, who are in the employ of the villainous Rastapopoulos. They land on a volcanic Indonesian island, where Rastapopoulos plans to use Dr Krollspell's truth serum to learn Carreidas' secret Swiss bank account number. However, the serum fails. Tintin and his friends escape and are chased by Rastapopoulos's henchman, Allan. They manage to take Carreidas back and flee into secret underground tunnels, guided by telepathic messages sent by the mysterious Mik Ezdanitoff (Mik Kanrokitoff). Kanrokitoff is the Earth agent of outer space aliens who landed on the island centuries earlier. The island's volcano awakens. Tintin and his friends are hypnotised by Kanrokitoff and rescued by a flying saucer. The villains, who had escaped in a lifeboat, are also hypnotised and abducted, while Tintin and his friends are left in their place, the memories of the adventure erased. They are rescued by a passing plane but have no clear recollection of their adventure, except for an alien artefact pocketed by Calculus on the island.

Characters: Flight 714 totally demystifies the character of Rastapopoulos. Gone is the criminal mastermind who made an impressive entrance at the end of *The Blue Lotus* and who moved his men across the world like pieces on a chessboard in *The Red Sea Sharks*. In this book, Rastapopoulos needs cash, fast. He has become a farcical villain who dresses in a ridiculous Texan outfit, not unlike a character from a *Pink Panther* movie. He is still a presence to be feared but he is no longer worthy of respect. As for Allan, the cunning, brutal henchman of *The Crab with the Golden Claws* has been replaced by a low-brow, buffoonish thug, desperate to please his boss.

The other character of note in the book is the reclusive, misanthropic billionaire, Laszlo Carreidas. Carreidas could have been a mere Scrooge-like caricature, and that would have been enough to carry the story, but Hergé makes him more than that: in truth, he is a villain to rival Rastapopoulos. The scene when the two men, under the influence of Dr Krollspell's serum, try to outdo each other by telling stories of their past misdeeds to see who is the worst evil genius is both funny and terrifying. Ultimately, there is no difference between the 'respectable' Carreidas and the 'outlaw' Rastapopoulos – who, in fact, was a respectable mogul in *Cigars of the Pharaoh*. At the top, the barriers between good and evil have crumbled.

Continuity: Piotr Skut, Rastapopoulos and Allan, last seen in *The Red Sea Sharks*, return. Jolyon Wagg and his family offer their comments on the heroes' television interview. Tintin remarks upon the similarities between the underground tunnels of the island and those of the Temple of the Sun.

Influences: Hergé's fascination with the supernatural and the paranormal, having reached a peak in *Tintin In Tibet*, now takes a detour towards a more scientific – if not more plausible – subgenre, that of visitations by so-called 'Ancient Astronauts' and the presence of 'Great Initiates' among us. This material is inspired and derived not only from Jacques Bergier's books – although

Bergier himself was never lurid or forthright about some of his speculations – but also from Robert Charroux, the French Erik Von Daniken.

Trivia: The character of Mik Kanrokitoff looks like, and is based on renowned French writer, journalist and renaissance man Jacques Bergier (1912–1978). He was a specialist on various occult and esoteric matters, ranging from alchemy to top secret military research, a former editor of the magazine *Planète* (called *Comète* in the French version and *Space Week* in the English one) and with Louis Pauwels, the author of the international best-seller *Le Matin des Magiciens* (*The Morning of the Magicians*, 1960).

The television presenter who interviews our heroes at the end of the book is a young *Tintin* fan called Jean Tauré, who had sent a picture of himself to Hergé and had asked if he could be shown shaking the Captain's hand in a future book. Hergé accommodated him on page 62.

Review: Flight 714 is something of a let-down but, after *Tintin In Tibet* and its antithesis *The Castafiore Emerald*, how could it not be? The story of *Tintin* is over, or rather is on autopilot, which is not inappropriate considering the theme of the book.

The sense of derision that permeated *The Castafiore Emerald* detracts from the believability of a book that tries to be a serious adventure. The story has its dramatic moments, reminiscent of *The Calculus Affair* or *The Red Sea Sharks*, but these are usually undercut by almost parodic scenes, usually involving Rastapopoulos – who behaves here in an increasingly manic fashion reminiscent of Herbert Lom's Commissioner Dreyfus in the *Pink Panther* films.

Then, we have the Deus Ex Machina device of Mik Kanrokitoff, not to mention the last-minute rescue by the aliens during the rather convenient, sudden volcanic eruption. Here the book hovers on the edge of what could have truly been a fantastic adventure: Tintin meeting real aliens and having an adventure in outer space! At the time of *2001: A Space Odyssey* and about ten years before *Star Wars* – what a concept! Like it or hate it, that would have been another memorable book, possibly topping the previous two.

Instead, like a horse who refuses to jump, Hergé shied away from the logical consequences of what he had conceived, preferring to fall back on the lame 'memory erasure' device, and show as little of the aliens as possible. The man who had shown the Beast of *The Black Island*, a giant spider on *The Shooting Star*, the magic of the ancient Incas and the Yeti, could not bring himself to deal with aliens. If there were to be ancient space visitors in the Tintin Universe, then Tintin ought to have confronted them, as he confronted every fantastic threat before. What this shows is Hergé's lack of confidence in his storytelling abilities and, ultimately, his own character's ability to convincingly carry that story to its logical conclusion.

(Interestingly, at the same time, in *Le Journal de Tintin*, writer Michel Greg and artist Eddy Paape had just embarked on the telling of the adventures of blond explorer Luc Orient who, with his friend Professor Hugo Kala, was meeting white-skinned alien visitors in a Lost Valley in the Orient and went on an inter-planetary adventure to rescue planet Terango.)

As a result, the first part of *Flight 714* – that deals with Carreidas's kidnapping – is undermined by its satirical elements, and the second part – that deals with the aliens – is abruptly brought to an end before it has time to mature. *Flight 714* ends up being a disappointing book in spite of its high promise. 3/5.

Tintin and the Picaros

Publishing History:

1. Serialisation in Belgium and in France in *Tintin-l'Hebdoptimiste* from September 1975 (Nos. 1–31).
2. *Tintin et les Picaros*, 62 pages, colour, Editions Casterman, Tournai, 1976.

Eight years elapsed between *Flight 714* and this story, the last completed *Tintin* adventure. When it was eventually published, it was panned by the critics – probably the first time ever – but did very well commercially.

Plot: The South American Republic of San Theodoros is again divided by civil strife. Propped up by the Bordurians, General Tapioca rules in Los Dopicos (renamed Tapiocapolis), while his rival, General Alcazar, financed by the International Banana Company, leads a guerrilla war in the jungle with his Picaros. In Marlinspike, Haddock is surprised to discover that he can no longer stand the taste of whisky. Then, the Castafiore and the Thompsons are arrested on spying charges in San Theodoros; Tapioca accuses

Tintin and his friends of co-conspiracy and taunts them to come to San Theodoros. Against Tintin's advice, Haddock and Calculus go, only to discover themselves prisoners of its police state; they are later joined by Tintin. The real villain is Bordurian Colonel Sponz, eager for revenge. Sponz plans to use Tintin to trap Alcazar but his plan fails. Our heroes team up with Alcazar, who is now married to Peggy and is staying with the Arumbayas. He is discouraged because his men have all become hopelessly drunk. They are cured by Calculus's new pill which he had secretly been testing on Haddock. While the Castafiore and the Thompsons are put on a mock trial, Tintin has the idea of infiltrating the city using Jolyon Wagg's Turlurons (Jolly Follies) troupe who have come for the Carnival. Alcazar's disguised men capture Tapioca and save the Thompsons from a firing squad. Much to his chagrin, Tapioca is merely exiled and Sponz is sent back to Borduria.

Characters: Alcazar's 'Last Hurrah' could have been the title of the book, which gives the ebullient general a last spotlight. But Alcazar, like the other characters, is a deflated version of what he used to be. Now married to the shrewish Peggy – who only he and Calculus seem to appreciate – he has become the hapless leader of a band of drunks. He has to disguise himself as a clown in order to retake power, and even then he is frustratingly denied his rightful revenge by Tintin. The last image we have of him is a prisoner in his own palace. A sad, yet somehow appropriate, ending.

Continuity: Tintin and the Picaros is a sequel of sorts to

Tintin and the Broken Ear. General Alcazar (last seen in *The Red Sea Sharks*) returns, as well as Pablo, explorer-gone-native Ridgewell and the Arumbayas from the earlier book. At last we discover the face of General Tapioca, a South American Mussolini. The villainous Sponz seeks to extract revenge for the humiliation he received in *The Calculus Affair*.

The Castafiore remains unflappable throughout the book, as if she alone could see it for the farce that it is. As the goddess of chaos, she is accompanied here by other minor chaos-generating imps, such as the Thompsons and Jolyon Wagg. It not surprising that the entire San Theodoros adventure starts and ends with them. There has been much agitation by all the other characters throughout the book but nothing has truly changed. The Castafiore stands unscathed. Maybe Haddock was right to fear her all that time...

Influences: Tintin and the Picaros was inspired by the adventure of real-life French left-wing intellectual Régis Debray who joined the guerrillas led by Che Guevara in Bolivia, and was later sentenced to 30 years in jail. Debray was released after three years because of the intervention of President de Gaulle, André Malraux and Jean-Paul Sartre. He returned to writing and his 1967 *Revolution In the Revolution* became a classic reference work on the subject of guerrillas.

Trivia: The Picaros were originally named 'Bigotudos.' For the first time, Tintin's wardrobe was updated, to better reflect the times. Gone are the gold pants, replaced by ordinary jeans. He is also shown practising yoga and wears a peace sign on his helmet.

Peggy, Alcazar's wife, was created by Hergé after watching a documentary on the KKK on television, which featured a woman with similar traits.

The carnival crowd drawn by Bob De Moor features guest appearances by other comic icons, such as Astérix and Mickey (page 54), Donald and Groucho Marx (page 59), and Snoopy (page 60).

Review: With *Tintin and the Picaros*, the *Tintin* franchise faced the same set of problems that the *James Bond* franchise experienced, and failed to solve them successfully.

Updating Tintin's clothes and showing him wearing a peace sign – which was already ten years out of date! – is just cosmetic dressing, to a large extent indicative of outmoded, surface thinking unable to grapple with the real issues. The problem lies with the fact that the world around the characters had changed and could no longer be handled or depicted as it once was. *The Picaros* only exacerbates the situation by choosing to focus on the real political problems of South America instead of some imaginary criminal conspiracy, yet deals with it in a fashion that totally lacks credibility.

The real San Theodoros of the mid-1970s, if it existed, would have been a vastly different and much bloodier country than the updated version of the comical San Theodoros of the mid-1930s that is on embarrassing display here. On the one hand, *Tintin and the Picaros* invites us to think about serious issues, such as guerrilla war, poverty and death squads; on the other hand, it gives us the Jolly Follies! *The Blue Lotus*, this isn't.

Like their creator, the characters seem tired: Tintin is totally reactive – even on the book cover, it is Haddock who takes the lead. In the end, Alcazar and Tapioca agree: good, old-fashioned traditions – in this case, executions! – have gone out of the window and they now live in sad times. That disillusionment is best on display in the last panel, which reprises a scene from page 11, and shows two policemen patrolling a *favella* – only the uniforms have changed; poverty remains. Tintin may have helped his friends – as he helped Emir Ben Kalish Ezab in Khemed – but in the end, he did not really change things. The hero is dead.

Graphically, the Hergé Studios, and the diligent Bob De Moor, took over maybe a little more of the art chores than they should have. The undefinable magic of the Hergé line that was still present in *Flight 714* is sometimes missing from *Tintin and the Picaros*. *Flight 714* was frustrating, but had promise. *Tintin and the Picaros* is just sad. 2/5.

Tintin and Alph-Art

Publishing History:
1. *Tintin et L'Alph-Art* (unfinished), Editions Casterman, Tournai, 1986.

Hergé began working on his last *Tintin* story in 1978. Originally entitled *Tintin et les Faussaires* (*Tintin and the Forgers*), he later changed the working title to *Tintin et L'Alph-Art*. As the story evolved, he also added a new element to the original plot about art forgers: that of a religious sect led by a deadly, phoney guru. Hergé died in March 1983 without resolving and completing the story, leaving about 150 pages of partly pencilled pages, lay-outs, and script notes – but no specific instructions as to what should be done in the event of his death.

It was first contemplated that *Alph-Art* would be finished by Bob De Moor. (De Moor later went on to finish Edgar P Jacobs' last, unfinished *Blake & Mortimer* story.) But ultimately, Hergé's widow, Fanny Rémi, decided against that option. Instead, the documents left by Hergé were sorted out and edited by a team of various experts, comprised among others of Benoît Peeters, Michel Bareau and Jean-Manuel Duvivier. The material was condensed to 42 comics pages, and presented in the form of a hardcover book containing on the left side an edited transcription of the script, and on the right side a facsimile reproduction of Hergé's pencils and lay-outs.

Tintin and Alph-Art was officially released on 8 October 1986 and, in spite of its high cover price, became a best-selling book.

Plot: While trying to escape the impending arrival of the Castafiore, Captain Haddock becomes acquainted with the world of art galleries and discovers artist Ramo Nash's so-called Alph-Art – giant letters made of various materials. Tintin later investigates the mysterious deaths of two art experts and escapes two attempts on his life. The trail leads to a new age guru, Endaddine Akass, and to the island of Ischia near Naples. There, Tintin discovers that Ramo Nash is secretly painting forgeries for Akass, who plans to use his influence to sell them to a coterie of international billionaires. Tintin is unmasked and is going to be killed by being turned into a fake César sculpture.

Characters: Hergé knew the world of art and was attuned to its colourful characters. If developed, the character of forger Ramo Nash may have been interesting to explore – a genuinely gifted artist, yet a huckster.

Continuity: It was revealed in an unpublished page that Endaddine Akass was, in reality, Rastapopoulos in disguise. One supposes that after erasing his memories of *Flight 714*, Mik Kanrokitoff just abandoned him somewhere. Rastapopoulos's wealthy victims included a Who's Who of the Tintin Universe: Emir Ben Kalish Ezab of Khemed (last seen in *The Red Sea Sharks*), Ivan Sakharine (from *The Secret of the Unicorn*), American businessmen Gibbons (from *The Blue Lotus*) and Chicklet (from *Tintin and the Broken Ear*).

Influences: The book was initially influenced by the real-life case of notorious Fernand Legros. A former ballet dancer, Legros sold the works of forgers Real Lessart and Elmyr de Hory, fooling many American millionaires, including Arthur Meadows, the owner of General American Oil of Texas. Legros used a clever stratagem to authenticate his forgeries. When asked by US customs what was in his luggage, he claimed that the paintings were copies. US customs officials would then call upon art experts to determine whether Legros was trying to cheat them and, driven by such suspicion, these specialists concluded that the paintings were genuine. Legros would pay the fine, but then was able

JEAN-MARC AND RANDY LOFFICIER

to show his customers an official customs document proving the authenticity of the works he was selling! Legros was eventually arrested, jailed and ultimately died from throat cancer a pauper.

The existence of phoney cults preying on wealthy victims were also in the air in the early 1980s, and found a logical place in the plot of *The Alph-Art*. Hergé had read an article (in *Paris-Match*!) about the so-called Maharajah Magesh, which provided the spark for the character of Endaddine Akass.

Trivia: Several unauthorised versions of *Tintin and Alph-Art*, one by the anonymous 'Ramo Nash' in 1987, several by Canadian artist Yves Rodier, then one by Regric etc. were distributed illegally by fans in the 1990s.

Review: It is naturally impossible to review an unfinished work, especially with so many variables not having been defined by Hergé. The only thing one can tell is that if the execution had been at least as professional as that of the previous volumes, *Tintin and Alph-Art* may have turned out to be a smaller-scale, unpretentious yet far more exciting and true-to-life adventure.

Tintin in the Media

Films and Television

(Note: We have replaced the original French titles by their English-language equivalent for straightforward book adaptations.)

A series of short 'films' made of black & white stills shot from the albums entitled *Les Films Fixes* were successfully exploited by the company *Les Beaux Films* during the war, but Hergé reportedly never saw any profits.

The Crab with the Golden Claws
Director/Writer: Claude Misonne and João B Michiels.
Voices: No information available. (colour, 75 mins, 1947)
  This was a stop-motion puppet film made by a small Belgian studio. The adaptation was faithful to the book, but not too impressive. 1/5.

Les Aventures de Tintin – Series I
1–6. *King Ottokar's Sceptre*; 7–12. *Tintin and the Broken Ear*.
  Director: Ray Goossens. *Voices*: Jean Nohain (Narrator). (black & white, twelve five-min episodes, 1956)

Produced by the Belgian animation studio Belvision, newly created by Raymond Leblanc, publisher of the *Journal de Tintin*, this first series was made as a test of the studio's abilities and of *Tintin*'s marketability to television. The animation was very limited, but the adaptations were faithful. Each book was cut into six five-minute episodes, broadcast daily in the form of a weekly serial. 2/5.

Les Aventures de Tintin – Series II
1. *Destination Moon*; 2. *Explorers on the Moon*; 3. *The Crab with the Golden Claws*; 4. *The Secret of the Unicorn*; 5. *Red Rackham's Treasure*; 6. *The Shooting Star*; 7. *The Black Island*; 8. *The Calculus Affair*.
Director: Ray Goossens. *Writer*: Michel Greg. (colour, ninety-one five-min episodes, 1957)

Produced by Belvision, again using limited animation, but in colour. Eight books were adapted in the same daily 5–minute episode format. Michel Greg is a famous Belgian comics writer/artist, and became editor-in-chief of the *Journal de Tintin* from 1965 to 1974. These look extremely dated by today's standards and the adaptations are often either too skimpy or downright unfaithful to the original material. 1/5.

Tintin et le Mystère de la Toison D'Or (Tintin And The Mystery of the Golden Fleece)
Director: Jean-Jacques Vierne. *Writers*: André Barret, Rémo Forlani. *Cast*: Jean-Pierre Talbot (Tintin), Georges Wilson (Haddock), Georges Loriot (Calculus), Demetrios Myri (Karabine), Charles Vanel (Father

Alexander), Dario Moreno (Midas Papos), Marcel Bozzuffi (Angorapoulos), Dimitrios Starenios (Scoubidovitch), Max Elloy (Nestor). (colour, 94 mins, 1961)

Plot: Haddock inherits the *Golden Fleece*, an old steamer from his late friend, Themistocle Paparanic. The ship is the key to a fortune in gold which Paparanic stole from a South American republic. The villainous Anton Karabine tries to steal the ship. Calculus uses the ship to test a pill which, when dropped in the fuel tank, makes the *Golden Fleece* go at incredible speeds. The gold is finally located, disguised as painted handrails.

First live action *Tintin* film, based on an original story. The casting is inspired, and the well-directed story captures the spirit of *Tintin*, although without the subtleties and multi-layered qualities of the comics. The Greek and Turkish locations add the required exotic note. 4/5.

Book: *Tintin and the Mystery of the Golden Fleece*, Editions Casterman, Tournai, 1962.

Tintin et les Oranges Bleues (Tintin and the Blue Oranges)
Director: Philippe Condroyer. *Writer*: André Barret. *Cast*: Jean-Pierre Talbot (Tintin), Jean Bouise (Haddock), Félix Fernandez (Calculus), Francky François, André Marie (Thompsons), Jenny Orléans (Castafiore), Angel Alvarez (Zalamea), Max Elloy (Nestor). (colour, 110 mins, 1964)

Plot: Spanish Professor Antenor Zalamea, a friend of Prof. Calculus, has succeeded in producing blue oranges that could grow in the desert and solve the world's hunger problems. The two scientists are kidnapped by an evil emir whose interests are threatened by this discovery. With the help of Spanish children, Tintin rescues the scientists.

Second live action film, based on an original story. The casting does not work as well: Talbot (as Tintin) is starting to look his age and Bouise (as Haddock) is not as good as Wilson. On the other hand, Jenny Orléans is a great Castafiore. The direction is not quite as dynamic and the story skews too young. 2/5.

Book: *Tintin and the Blue Oranges*, Editions Casterman, Tournai, 1965.

Tintin and the Temple of the Sun
Director: Eddie Lateste. *Writers*: Michel Greg, Eddie Lateste, Jos Marissen, Laszló Molnár. *Voices*: Jacques Careuil (Tintin), Henri Virlojeux (Haddock), Jacques Balutin (Prof. Calculus). (colour, 80 mins, 1969)

Belvision's first full-length *Tintin* animated feature. The animation is better, but not quite up to international standards. The adaptation is good, although *The Seven Crystal Balls* portion of the story suffers from being overly condensed for timing reasons. The music by François Rauber is excellent. Zorrino's song was composed by renowned singer/composer Jacques Brel. A new character was added: Maita, the Inca's daughter, who befriended Zorrino. 3/5.

Tintin et le Lac aux Requins (Tintin and the Lake of Sharks)
Director: Raymond Leblanc. *Writers:* Michel Greg, Eddie Lateste, Jos Marissen, Jean-Michel Charlier, Rainer Gocksch. *Voices:* Jacques Careuil (Tintin), Henri Virlojeux (Haddock), Jacques Balutin (Prof. Calculus). (colour, 75 mins, 1972)

Plot: Calculus has invented a three-dimensional duplicating machine, which he is testing near a lake in Syldavia. Rastapopoulos, aka King Shark, tries to steal it. Tintin outwits his old foe with the help of two local children, Nino and Nouchka.

Belvision's second full-length *Tintin* animated feature, this time based on an original story. For some inexplicable reason, while the animation is undeniably better and the overall look richer, this film is less convincing than its predecessor. The original story is flat and manages to look uninspired by juxtaposing too many elements taken from different books: the shark submarine, a *Destination Moon*-like opening, Rastapopoulos, the Bordurians and even concepts from *Jo, Zette & Jocko*. 2/5.

Book: Tintin and the Lake of Sharks, Editions Casterman, Tournai, 1973. This book is made up of stills from the film assembled in the form of a comic book. An earlier adaptation of the story, drawn entirely as a traditional comic by Bob De Moor and the Hergé Studios, was serialised as a daily black & white strip in the Belgian newspaper *Le Soir* but was never officially collected in book form.

Les Aventures de Tintin
1. *Tintin In America*; 2. *Cigars of the Pharaoh*; 3. *The Blue Lotus*; 4. *Tintin and the Broken Ear*; 5. *The Black Island*; 6. *King Ottokar's Sceptre*; 7. *The Crab with the Golden Claws*; 8. *The Shooting Star*; 9. *The Secret of the Unicorn*; 10. *Red Rackham's Treasure*; 11. *The Seven Crystal Balls*; 12. *Prisoners of the Sun*; 13. *Land of Black Gold*; 14. *Destination Moon*; 15. *Explorers on the Moon*; 16. *The Calculus Affair*; 17. *The Red Sea Sharks*; 18. *Tintin In Tibet*; 19. *The Castafiore Emerald*; 20. *Flight 714*; 21. *Tintin and the Picaros*.

Director: Stéphane Bernasconi. *Writers*: Various. *Voices*: Thierry Wermuth (Tintin), Christian Pelissier (Haddock), Henri Labussière (Tournesol). (colour, twenty-one 42–min episodes, 1991)

Animated series produced by French studio Ellipse teamed up with Canadian animation company Nelvana. The adaptations are generally faithful, to the point of using compositions taken from actual comics panels in their storyboards. The pacing is brisk, and the animation acceptable, considering the limitations of a television budget. To the extent that it is possible to animate *Tintin* at all – an arguable proposition – this is likely to remain the best version for a long time. 4/5.

The Adventures of Tintin: Secret of the Unicorn
Director/Producer: Steven Spielberg, Peter Jackson. *Writers*: Steven Moffat, Edgar Wright, Joe Cornish. *Music*: John Williams. *Voices*: Jamie Bell (Tintin), Andy Serkis (Captain Haddock), Daniel Craig (Red Rackham), Simon Pegg (Inspector Thompson), Nick

Frost (Thompson). (colour, 2011)

Plot: A treasure hunt commences when Tintin and Snowy find directions to the sunken ship of Captain Haddock's ancestor. Tintin determines to solve a riddle that may lead to the treasure of Red Rackham the pirate.

This Tintin movie is entirely animated and uses motion capture, a technique that uses actors as a starting point to create a photorealistic animated film. Released in both 2D and 3D.

Books: The Crab with the Golden Claws, Editions Casterman, 1941. *The Secret of the Unicorn*, serialised in *Le Soir* from 11 June, 1942, Editions Casterman, 1943. *Red Rackham's Treasure*, Editions Casterman, 1944.

Stage

Tintin aux Indes – Le Mystère du Diamant Bleu (Tintin In India – The Mystery of the Blue Diamond)

Stage play in three acts by Hergé and Jacques Van Melkebeke.

Director: Paul Riga. *Cast:* Jeanne Rubens (Tintin), Marcel André, 'Mickey' (Thompsons). Théâtre des Galeries, Brussels, April 15 & 17, May 1 & 8, 1941.

Plot: Tintin investigates the disappearance of the Maharajah of Padhakore's Blue Diamond. The second act takes place aboard the ship *Rampura*. He will finally solve the mystery in the third act, in a castle in Syldavia.

This play was written in collaboration with journalist/friend Jacques Van Melkebeke who reportedly assisted Hergé in the plotting of a number of his books, and later became the first editor-in-chief of the *Journal de Tintin*. Strangely, the Dupond/t (Thompsons) are called Durant/d. Tintin was played by a young girl.

M. Boullock a Disparu (The Disappearance of Mr Boullock)
Stage play in three acts by Hergé and Jacques van Melkebeke.
Director: Paul Riga. *Cast*: Roland Ravez (Tintin), Marcel André, Robert Tournay (Thompsons). Théâtre des Galeries, Brussels, December 26, 29, 30, 1941, and January 3, 8, 1942.

Plot: Tintin, Snowy and the Thompsons chase after the mysterious Mr Boullock from Brussels to Casablanca, Argentina, China and Tibet, before returning to Belgium.

Second stage play collaboration with Van Melkebeke; this time the Thompsons are correctly named.

Audio

Les Aventures de Tintin (Radio-Luxembourg, 1950)
No information available.

Les Aventures de Tintin (Radio-Luxembourg, 1955)
Writer: Paul Achard. *Voices*: Claude Vincent (Tintin), Jean-Marie Amato (Haddock), Maurice Chevit (Tournesol).

Les Aventures de Tintin (Radio-Luxembourg, 1958)
Writer: Georges Vittel. *Voices*: Claude Vincent (Tintin), Jean-Marie Amato (Haddock), Guy Pierauld (Tournesol).

Les Aventures de Tintin (RTF, 1959)
Directors: René Wilmet, Jean Desforgues. *Writers*: Nicole Strauss, Jacques Langeais. *Voices*: Maurice Sarfati (Tintin), Jacques Hifling (Haddock), Jacques Dufilho (Tournesol).

The episodes *Prisoners of the Sun* (including *The Seven Crystal Balls*) and *Destination Moon* (including *Explorers on the Moon*) were reissued as two record albums by Pathé Records in 1965.

Les Aventures de Tintin (Europe 1, 1964)
Voices: Maurice Sarfati (Tintin), Jacques Hifling (Haddock), Jacques Dufilho (Tournesol).

Tintin Journals

Le Journal de Tintin
Published weekly in Belgium by Editions du Lombard and weekly in France by Editions Dargaud.

Belgian edition: first issue: 26 September 1946; last issue: 29 November 1988, when it was replaced by *Tintin Reporter*.

French edition: first issue: 28 October 1948; last issue: 28 December 1972, when it was replaced by *Tintin l'Hebdoptimiste*.

Publisher: Raymond Leblanc. Editors included Jacques Van Melkebeke, André Fernez, Marcel Dehaye, Michel Greg, Henri Desclez, André-Paul Duchateau and Jean-Luc Vernal.

Publisher Raymond Leblanc had the idea of creating a weekly children's magazine using the *Tintin* name to compete with *Spirou* and *Bravo*, and created the Editions du Lombard. First editor-in-chief Van Melkebeke was invited to resign soon after the magazine's launch because of his past association with Nazi-controlled *Le Soir*. He was replaced by writer André Fernez, the author of a popular series of juvenile spy thrillers, *Nick Jordan*. In 1965, Leblanc hired Michel Greg to take over. Greg's more modern approach to comics alienated Hergé, who distanced himself from the magazine; however, sales climbed up sharply from 100,000 to 150,000. Greg left in 1974, ending what is now considered the 'silver age' era of French comics magazines.

Tintin l'Hebdoptimiste
Published weekly in France by Editions Dargaud.
First issue: 9 January 1973; last issue: No. 140, 9 September 1975, when it was replaced by *Nouveau Tintin*.

Nouveau Tintin
Published weekly in France by Edi-Monde, then Ifford, then Cinq Pouce, then Lombard-France.
First issue: 16 September 1975; last issue: No. 142, 30 May 1978.

Tintin Spécial
Published quarterly in France by Cinq Pouce, then Lombard-France.
First issue: June 1978; last issue: No. 37, September 1989.

Tintin Reporter
Published weekly in France and Belgium by Yeti-Presse.

First issue: 9 December 1988; last issue: No. 34, 28 July 1989, when it became *Hello Bédé*.

Hello Bédé
Published weekly in France and Belgium by Editions du Lombard.

First issue: 26 September 1989; last issue: No. 197, 29 June 1993.

Reference Materials

In English:

Farr, Michael. *Tintin, The Complete Companion*. John Murray, 2001.

Peeters, Benoît. *Tintin and the World of Hergé – An Illustrated History*. Methuen, 1989.

Peeters, Benoît. *The Making of Tintin* (3 vols). Methuen, 1983–89.

Thompson, Harry. *Tintin: Hergé & His Creation*. Hodder and Stoughton, 1991.

In French:

Assouline, Pierre. *Hergé*. Plon, 1998.

Baetens, Jan. *Hergé Ecrivain*. Editions Labor, 1989.

Bonfand, Alain & Marion, Jean-Luc. *Hergé*. Hachette, 1996.

Dayez, Hugues. *Tintin et les Héritiers*. Editions du Félin/Éditions Luc Pire, 2000.

Farr, Michael. *Tintin – Le Rêve et la Réalité*. Editions Moulinsart, 2001.

Fresnault-Deruelle, Pierre. *Hergé ou le Secret de L'Image*. Editions Moulinsart, 1999.

Goddin, Philippe. *L'Aventure du Journal Tintin*. Editions du Lombard, 1986.

Goddin, Philippe. *Hergé et Tintin, Reporters du Petit Vingtième au Journal Tintin*. Editions du Lombard, 1986.

Goddin, Philippe. *Les Débuts D'Hergé: Du Dessin à la Bande Dessinée*. Editions Moulinsart, 1999.

Goddin, Philippe. *Hergé – Chronologie D'Une Oeuvre* (2 vols). Editions Moulinsart, 2000–01.

Lerman, Alain. *Histoire du Journal Tintin*. Editions Glénat, 1979.

Peeters, Benoît. *Le Monde D'Hergé*. Editions Casterman, 1983.

Peeters, Benoît. *Hergé, 1922–1932. Les Débuts D'Un Illustrateur*. Editions Casterman, 1987.

Sadoul, Numa. *Tintin et Moi – Entretiens Avec Hergé*. Editions Casterman, 1975.

Serres, Michel. *Hergé Mon Ami*. Editions Moulinsart, 2000.

Serres, Michel. *Tintin, Grand Voyageur du Siècle*. Editions Moulinsart, 2001.

Smolderen, Thierry & Sterckx, Pierre. *Hergé – Portrait Biographique*. Editions Casterman, 1988.

Steemans, Stéphane. *Tout Hergé – Itinéraire D'Un Collectionneur Chanceux*. Editions Casterman, 1991.

Tisseron, Serge. *Hergé*. Seghers, 1987.

Tisseron, Serge. *Tintin Chez le Psychanalyste*. Aubier, 1999.

Tisseron, Serge. *Tintin et le Secret D'Hergé*. Editions Presses de la Cité, 1993.

Vandromme, Paul. *Le Monde de Tintin*. Editions

Gallimard, 1959, rev. 1994.

Van Opstal, H. *Tracé RG – Le Phénomène Hergé*. Editions
Claude Lefrancq, 1999.

Websites:

La Fondation Hergé (Official Site) –
http://www.tintin.com

À La Découverte de Tintin –
www.free-tintin.net

Hergé & Tintin (in English) -
www.members.tripod.com/~thunderlizard/
tintin.html

Marlinspike Hall (in English) –
www.remick.net/tintin

Tintin's Parodies – http://perso.orange.fr/prad

Tintin's Webring
 – http://o.webring.com/hub?ring=tintinring

Index